Appraising and Exploring Organisations

First published in 1988, this book offers a comprehensive description of the functions and performance of organisational surveys from a wide range of European experts in the field.

The book examines the utility of organisational surveys as a method of research for the social sciences and as a support for employee relations strategies and personnel policies. It looks at the broad question of 'what are the key dimensions of an organisation with which managers and researchers should be concerned?' and at how they can be an essential element in a participative management approach to employee relations. Throughout, the book emphasizes the utility of surveys for the study and understanding of organisations.

T0299938

Appraising and Exploring Organisations

Edited by
S. Tyson,
K. F. Ackermann,
M. Domsch and
P. Joynt

Routledge
Taylor & Francis Group

First published in 1988
by Croom Helm Ltd

This edition first published in 2011 by Routledge
2 Park Square, Milton Park, Abingdon, Oxon, OX14 4RN

Simultaneously published in the USA and Canada
by Routledge
711 Third Avenue, New York, NY 10017

Routledge is an imprint of the Taylor & Francis Group, an informa business

Publisher's Note
The publisher has gone to great lengths to ensure the quality of this reprint but
points out that some imperfections in the original copies may be apparent.

Disclaimer
The publisher has made every effort to trace copyright holders and welcomes
correspondence from those they have been unable to contact.

A Library of Congress record exists under ISBN: 0709943407

ISBN 13: 978-0-415-69986-0 (hbk)
ISBN 13: 978-0-203-12711-7 (ebk)

Appraising and Exploring Organisations

Edited by S. TYSON, K.F. ACKERMANN,
M. DOMSCH and P. JOYNT

CROOM HELM
London ● New York ● Sydney

© 1988 S. Tyson, K.F. Ackermann, M. Domsch and P. Joynt
Croom Helm Ltd, Provident House, Burrell Row,
Beckenham, Kent, BR3 1AT
Croom Helm Australia, 44-50 Waterloo Road,
North Ryde, 2113, New South Wales

Published in the USA by
Croom Helm
in association with Methuen, Inc.
29 West 35th Street
New York, NY 10001

British Library Cataloguing in Publication Data

Appraising and exploring organisations.
  1. Organisation — Research
  I. Tyson, S.
  302.3'5   HM131
ISBN 0-7099-4340-7

Library of Congress Cataloging-in-Publication Data
ISBN 0-7099-4340-7

Printed and bound in Great Britain
by Billing & Sons Limited, Worcester.

CONTENTS

Personnel Policies

CONTRIBUTORS

K F Ackermann	University of Stuttgart
D Ashton	University of Lancaster
R Bouwen	Katholieke Industriële Hogeschool, Belgium
A Bowey	Consultant,
G de Cock	Katholieke Industriële Hogeschool, Belgium
P Conrad	Freie Universität Berlin
M Domsch	Universität der Bundeswehr Hamburg
B Geens	Vrije Universiteit Brussel
B W Hennestad	Norwegian School of Management
P Joynt	Bedriftsøkonomisk Institutt, Norway
F Nijhuis	University of Limburg
E Rosseel	Vrije Universiteit Brussel
A Schneble	Universität der Bundeswehr Hamburg
J Sveters	University of Limburg
J Sydow	Freie Universität Berlin

S Tyson   Cranfield Institute of
               Technology, England

J de Visch   Katholieke Industriële
               Hogeschool, Belgium

K de Witte   Katholieke Industriële
               Hogeschool, Belgium

Chapter One

INTRODUCTION

K F Ackermann, M Domsch, P Joynt, A Schneble and
S Tyson

"Man is the measure of all things" Protagoras 481 -
411 BC

This book takes as its subject the process by which
organisational life is measured. The techniques
adopted for this purpose do not measure things but
measure people. At one level, our discussion of
organisation survey methods concerns how to discover
data about employees through various investigative
techniques. However, since it is not possible to have
a complete knowledge of human beings, given the
complexities of behaviour and relationships, any
attempt to measure variables such as employee
attitudes, "morale" or feelings is fraught with
difficulty. The themes addressed by this book are the
appropriate methodologies for studying the varied
phenomena of organisational life, the validity of
survey techniques, and the value of surveys. In this
chapter, we will introduce these themes which recur
throughout the book. In addition, any serious
discussion of how "facts" are discovered must
recognise, as the Hawthorne experiments found so many
years ago, that the facts include the behaviour and
attitudes of the researchers as well as the researched
(Roethlisberger and Dickson 1939). Consequently we
will at the outset accept the volatile environment of
organisation politics, in which meanings are
negotiated and acknowledge that results from surveys,
however pure the methodology, become a part of the
environment being researched.

Organisation surveys are initiated for a variety of
reasons. Managers are most likely to want to gather
data, but trade unionists, social scientists,
government agencies, and market researchers amongst
others may also wish to gather information. Our book
is aimed primarily at managers and those who study
organisations. Managers perhaps have a greater need
than others because of the distance that has developed

1

between employees and those in control, but they usually also have the power and resources to initiate enquiries. Our reasons for presenting this collection of papers are to assist those who wish to undertake organisation surveys, or to interpret the results, whether they be practising managers, or social scientists, who, like us, are concerned with appraising and exploring organisations.

Accelerating technical and social change causes a growing need for information. On the one hand it is of great importance to be able to describe and interpret exactly the relationships, which result from the behaviour and the cooperation of employees. Only in this way can personnel management shape the working conditions, the organisation structure and climate effectively. On the other hand companies have to scrutinise continuously the organisation's structure to identify weaknesses so they may take corrective action. Organisational surveys can be used to gather all the necessary information, if they are conducted regularly and intensively. In this sense, surveys have to be considered as an integral tool of personnel management.

Surveys can therefore serve the research, analysis and prediction needs of personnel staff. Furthermore surveys can provide the start of an organisational development process, if the results of analysis (for example, into work attitudes, supervisory styles, informal structures and organisational climate) are evaluated and followed by strategies and steps to improve personnel management.

A number of the papers presented here argue that surveys are able to do more than just gather information. One goal of corporate leadership is to satisfy the demand for participation of both the indirect and the direct kind.

Surveys which enable the members of an organisation to express their attitudes anonymously, show one representative picture of the large number of personal views. Each subordinate is able to express his or her opinion of the working situation directly and free of any fear or constraint.

A comparison with the company's marketing policy, where continuous marketing research is conducted outside the organisation shows distinctly that internal market research of the employees is necessary and meaningful. The subordinates are the "customers" and "partners" in the enterprise. Hence the decisions on necessary action, plans for changes, which concern the employees and their working situation, should be brought about by the corporate leadership, with management and work people acting together. Such an organisational development process can best be achieved by participative decision-making. The employees are the best experts on their work situation.

Surveys as a mechanism for concerted decisions depend upon the following aspects, to become reality:

1. There must be a good opportunity for each employee to express honestly and critically attitudes towards their own work and to the corporate and personnel policy in general.

2. Subsequent to the survey there must be participative decisions on actions and strategies inside the company.

3. Surveys should not contain any form of sanctions.

If these conditions are not realised, surveys are no help for superiors and subordinates as partners, but only provide "pseudo-participation".

We must also recognise that organisation surveys are an important management tool in control terms. Managers are able to deepen and to reconsider their knowledge and understanding of their subordinates' interests and attitudes. After the analysis of the survey and following discussion of the results, managers are able to recognise the degree of work satisfaction, and satisfaction with the management, the corporate goals and policy in general. Regular organisation surveys enable comparison between current and former surveys to be made, so that changes are monitored over a period of time. If changes and improvements are researched and evaluated continuously, there is the possibility of correcting and varying the actions accordingly.

We will now consider the crucial question, how valid are organisation surveys?

INTRODUCTION

1. Validity and other requirements to surveys

Surveys have to meet special requirements in order to
be useful as a human resource management tool. Among
these requirements, the following are of outstanding
importance: validity and, in addition, reliability and
objectivity. They indicate the quality standard of a
survey.

In the social sciences, the validity of a test
indicates whether and to what extent this test really
measures what it should measure (Brandstätter (1970);
Attestlander (1975); Mayntz et al. (1978); Kromrey
(1980); Töpfer and Zander (1985).

If a survey is designed as a special test to measure,
say, the organisational climate or satisfaction and
dissatisfaction of the workers in a company, validity
would mean then, that the organisation climate or
satisfaction and dissatisfaction are really measured
by the underlying questionnaire. Obviously, surveys
with low validity could be very misleading as a basis
for management decisions. The goal, therefore, is or
should be to apply surveys which show high validity.

Another important criterion of the quality standard of
a survey is its reliability. In general, reliability
indicates how well or badly a specific variable is
measured by the test applied. It should be noticed
that the reliability of a survey might be high, while
at the same time its validity is rather low. However,
high reliability is always necessary to reach high
validity.

The third quality criterion mentioned above was
objectivity. The greater the objectivity, the more
its results are independent of the person who has
executed the test. Sometimes, objectivity is called
"interrater-reliability" and interpreted as a special
aspect of reliability. Like all other aspects of
reliability high objectivity or interrater reliability
is a pre-requisite for high validity.

2. Types of Validity

Several different types of validity need to be
distinguished. The main types are: content validity,
construct validity and criteria validity.

4

a)   Content Validity

The content validity of a survey derives from the thesis that the survey and its test elements represent the variable which is and should be measured.   This thesis is either based on logical considerations or on expert ratings.   Therefore, content validity is also called "face validity" or "expert validity."

A survey designed to measure the success of a training course in terms of knowledge increase has content validity if it is proven that the various tasks of the test adequately refer to the training programme (Lienert 1967).   Another example of content validity is provided by a survey which is directed to the measurement of work satisfaction and dissatisfaction in a sample of workers.   The questions asked in the survey evoke feelings of satisfaction and/or dissatisfaction, which are to be measured   (Neuberger 1983).   From this point of view, the survey can be said to have content validity.

Most organisational surveys rely heavily on content validity.

b)   Construct Validity

Construct validity exists if the survey and its test elements cover the essential characteristics of the theoretical "construct" which is to be measured.   The "construct", for example organisational climate, organisational commitment, work satisfaction and dissatisfaction etc., determines the structure of the survey, while survey results may modify the underlying construct.

For constructs like those mentioned above various questionnaires exist which claim more or less construct validity.   In these cases, organisational surveys will tend to apply already proven and accepted questionnaires.   If no questionnaire exists or reasons require a company-tailored one, the problem is how the construct validity of the newly developed tests can be determined.

Methods to determine construct validity of a survey include (Lienert 1967):

1)   The correlation of survey results with the results from other surveys applying different

questionnaires for the measurement of the same construct. High correlations would point to a reasonable construct validity, provided that the comparison surveys are valid themselves.

2) The intercorrelation of the individual items used in the questionnaire. As all items are related to the same construct, the intercorrelation coefficients of the variables should be high.

3) Analysis of survey results in different samples. Different results should be consistent with the construct under study and the assumptions derived from it.

These and other methods are complementary. There is no measure for the extent of construct validity.

c) Criteria Validity

Criteria validity of a survey exists if this survey and its test elements are closely related with one or several accepted validity criteria. The existing relationship between the survey results and the criteria are mostly measured by correlation coefficients. High (low) correlations indicate high (low) criteria validity. As these correlations are computed on the basis of empirical research data, criteria validity is sometimes called empirical validity as opposed to content and construct validity. The selection of a suitable validity criterion may be a difficult problem. It is solved according to the goals of the respective survey. For example, a survey designed to measure work satisfaction and dissatisfaction of workers might use widely accepted manifestations of satisfaction and dissastisfaction as validity criteria. Such criteria are, for example absenteeism and turnover. The majority of researchers suggest, that decreasing the work satisfaction of workers will increase their absenteeism and turnover. The conclusion then is that a valid survey on work satisfaction should produce results which are negatively correlated with the criteria (absenteeism and/or turnover) on a statistically significant level.

Two types of criteria validity are distinguished: "predictive validity" and "concurrent validity". Predictive validity relates survey results to

future criteria measures. In the example
mentioned above, high predictive validity would
mean that the survey results on work satisfaction
are highly and negatively correlated with the
future rate of absenteeism and/or turnover.
Concurrent validity relates survey results to
criteria measures which are computed in the same
time period.

3.   How much validity is necessary?

There is no general rule regarding the minimum
extent of validity required for a survey. In
principle, the greater the validity a survey has,
the better for decision-making this will be.
However, as we are living in an early stage of
organisational survey applications as a
management tool, aspiration levels as to the
quality standard of such surveys should not be
unreasonably high.

The validity of a survey will be restricted to
content validity only where the data cannot be
measured in quantitative terms and the researcher
relies more or less on the result of expert
ratings. Construct validity and even more
criteria validity are widely neglected in the
present company practice of survey applications.
The social sciences suggest that a test should be
valid to such an extent that its application
allows better forecasts than its omission
(Leinert 1967). This is also true for
organisational surveys. Organisational surveys
are at present more often designed for diagnostic
than for predictive purposes and their results
serve as supplementary information for decision-
making in addition to other information. Our
conclusion is that surveys might be allowed to
have a lower validity than is required in other
fields of test applications. Without
exaggerating the methodological requirements in
regard to test validity, organisational surveys
can play an important role as a human resource
management tool of the company.

So far in this chapter we have identified the
functions, needs and validity of surveys. We will now
concentrate on the outcomes and value of surveys.

INTRODUCTION

The Utility/Value of Surveys

We are specifically interested in what surveys can do
for an organisation both in the short-run and the
long-run. Performance and productivity improvement
are closely related to these outcomes and values, as
are such concepts as organisation change, organisation
development, organisation dynamics and organisation
renewal.

The classic analogy of a driver looking out of the
back window while driving not only fits the planning
function of management but also the functions
connected with surveys. Possibly the most important
aspect of surveys is to give managers an idea of
where they are. An added plus would be to know where
the organisation has been and there are some companies
who have begun to use continual surveys in this
context. However, most of the organisations we have
had contact with still use the single survey.

Value of Surveys

The most important value gained by the use of surveys
is the attention that is often given to the task,
information, human concern and management matrix. We
are well beyond the period where single solutions were
taught in management schools and the new trends in
management and organisation learning call for a more
detailed analysis of the "situation at hand". Surveys
can accomplish this, and they often give the
organisation the necessary insights to make changes or
adjust the course of action before it is too late.

A second value to be gained by survey efforts is the
attention to process or "how things are done here".
At times managers have a tendency to focus on the new
techniques of the day or to go too far with an MIS
system, operations research, CAD/CAM, project, or for
example in using one technique such as transactional
analysis, in training. A survey affords the
opportunity to assess the value of some of these
techniques as they effect the overall process of
management. The process can then be changed and
adapted to improve performance and productivity.

A third value involves the attention given to short-
run decisions versus long-run planning. Many managers
wear blinkers and have a difficult time thinking in
the long-run. Surveys often provide the necessary

impulses for a good long-run solution involving planning and a new mode of management thinking.

A fourth value can be labelled the acceptance of the need for some type of diagnosis as the first step in a successful change process. Again the idea of diagnosis, continual if possible, is closely related to the idea that there is no one best way to manage or organise. These developments are often called situational management or contingency theory in management and organisation literature and one returns to the classic case history methodology in order to find out what is happening.

Finally, as we have outlined above the survey is a very democratic instrument. It asks for the individual reaction on a variety of well-known organisation variables such as task, human relations, information as well as communications, decision-making, planning, job design, internal and external environment, culture, changed tempo, structure, policy, etc. One's imagination is the only limitation here.

Organisational Effectiveness

Organisational effectiveness encompasses a broad range of management and organisation goals. Steers (1975) and Joynt (1979) have attempted to summarise these as follows:

effectiveness	-	getting the job done
efficiency	-	optimal use of resources (INPUT/OUTPUT)
innovation	-	new ideas
satisfaction	-	a good job
security	-	both in terms of employment and health
growth	-	progress
survival	-	staying in "business"

Surveys play an important role in achieving both the short-term and long-term activities connected with these goals. In a general sense the survey is often the first step of a rather detailed change process as shown over in Figure 1.

Figure 1   The Survey Process

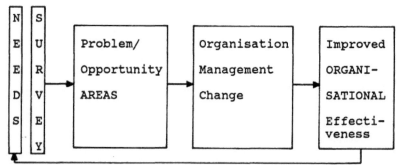

Since the needs (shown in Figure 1) are often a result
of conflicts, problems or opportunities with
organisational and managerial performance it might be
wise to review this in terms of survey methodology.
Many of the examples will be found in this book. The
survey-organisational effectivenesss interface is
shown in Figure 2.   As a point of reference the
authors use the concepts of organisational
effectiveness and organisational productivity
interchangeably.   We also view managerial performance
as an essential part of organisational performance.

Our interface figure shows that the questionnaire is
still the most widely used type of survey technique.
This might be due to the state of the art.   The
literature as well as this book tends to show that
the survey is often used to solve short-term (one year
or less) conflicts and problems; few organisations
have adopted a long-term multitime period perspective.
Shell, IBM, Phillips, and some of the large Japanese
firms are the exceptions here and their numbers are
growing.

As a summary of our description of surveys Figure 2
may be used as a starting point for integrating the
aspects of organisational effectivness, managerial and
organisational behaviour, and survey needs in those
diagnostic long-term activities which will improve
organisational performance.

The Structure of the Book

The papers presented in this book span a
representative range of survey purposes and
techniques.   They include the study of organisations
as cultural wholes using a semiotic approach, standard

questionnaire techniques to discover attitudes to change, psychometric measures of managerial training needs, and action learning approaches to organisation development. As well as the reflective papers which discuss and compare techniques, the collection has a pan European style which is intended to assist cross-cultural comparisons. The book is divided into three parts: organisation "culture", employee relations and personnel policies. One of the reasons for adopting this structure is because we believe by showing the papers in juxtaposition to each other, different approaches are illustrated to the solution of similar problems. This illuminates the relationship between the problem and the methodology with which it was explored. This we believe is a key issue which emerges from the book.

In the section on organisation culture the chapters consider the theoretical and practical issues raised when undertaking surveys of organisation "culture" or "climate". Conrad and Sydow outline the methodological consequences of a perceptual approach to organisational climate and clarify the advantages and disadvantages of traditional approaches to measurement. The following paper considers organisational climate as a general notion specifying the self image of the organisation where de Cock, Bouwen, de Witte and de Visch describe a model of competing organisational values, along the dimensions of flexibility/control and organisation/people. Hennestad takes a large company in Norway as a case study to demonstrate how an organisation can be conceived as a separate "ideational system" by means of a study of the symbols of the organisation. In this sense, Hennestad uses a semiotic approach. The creating and recreating forces which create this living history are seen to reside in contradictions constituted by its multi cultural reality, as well as the contradiction between culture and social structure.

The papers in the section on employee relations are concerned with how surveys can be used both to discover the realities of employee attitudes, and as an essential element in participative management approaches. Ackermann argues that if properly designed and implemented, organisation surveys will improve management efficiency and effectiveness. He goes on to see how results can be turned into action, based on research into German companies. Domsch looks at employee attitude surveys in practice in an analysis of 24 companies, and examines what has to be done with regard to the decision power of employees, in order to utilise surveys as participative management tools. Following the previous paper, Soeters and Nijhuis compare and contrast two main methods of studying organisations: the questionnaire and the institutional approach. They explain the variation of results between the two measures by reference to the theoretical and practical weaknesses of these approaches, illustrating their views by a study of the quality of working life in 51 organisations in the Netherlands. Rosseel and Geens are able to take the debate on managing change further by investigating attitudes to the introduction of new technology.

In the section on personnel policies, the use of surveys as a tool to create, modify or monitor personnel policies is described by reference to policies on management development, career planning and pay and motivation. Ashton shows how to conduct a management development audit, which will support strategic decisions on management education, and Tyson looks at techniques which can be deployed to discover managerial competencies, and to analyse training needs drawing on UK experience. Joynt's chapter examines the methodology strategies used in the study of behaviour in a management career, using action learning techniques on a Norwegian project. We conclude with a paper by Bowey who reports on her research into UK engineering and shipbuilding companies' pay policies, where her survey, taking a contingency view of pay, enabled her to identify the variables which condition pay policy.

A major theme which emerges therefore is that organisation surveys perform vital functions within organisations, as a means of gathering crucial information about employees and relationships, and about the efficacy of personnel policies. An essential part of our understanding of what is happening is our ability to grasp what are the elements of each organisation's culture or "climate" in which relationships and policies are enacted.

Figure 2 Type of Surveys and Organisational
Effectiveness

Organisational effectiveness (goal criteria) / Type of Survey	effectiveness	efficiency	innovation	satisfaction	security	growth	survival
Questionnaire	E	E	S	E	S	S	S-N
Closed interview	S	S	S	S	N-S	S	S-N
Open interview	S	N	S	S	N-S	S	S
Case	S	S	E	N-S	N-S	S	S
Action learning programme	S	S	S	N-S	N-S	S	N-S
Secondary Data	S	S	S	N-S	N-S	S	S
National Data	S	S	N-S	N-S	N-S	S	S
World Data	S	S	N	N	N-S	S	S

E = extensively used
S = sometimes used
N = seldom (not used)

13

INTRODUCTION

References

Atteslander, P: Methoden der empirischen
    Sozialforschung, Wien/New York 1975.

Brandstätter, H: Die Beurteilung von Mitarbeitern,
    in: Mayer,A and Herwig, B (Hrsg.), Handbuch der
    Psychologie, Bd. 9, Betriebspsychologie, Göttingen
    1970, S. 668-734.

Joynt, P: A Norwegian empirical investigation into
    the theories and practices of administrative
    behaviour. Brunel University 1979.

Kromrey, H: Empirische Sozialforschung, Oplanden 1980.

Lienert, G A: Testaufbau und Testanalyse, 2. Aufl.
    Weinheim/Berlin 1967 (3. Aufl. 1969).

Mayntz, R et al: Einführung in die Methoden der
    empirischen Soziologie, Opladen 1978.

Neuberger, O: Der Arbeitsbeschreibungsbogen, Goch
    1983.

Roethlisberger, F J and Dickson W J: Management and
    the worker Cambridge Mass Harvard 1939.

Steers R M Problems in measurement of organisational
    effectiveness 1975 p.20.

Töpfer, A U and Zander, E (Hrsg.): Mitarbeiter
    befragungen, Frankfurt a.m./New York 1985.

Chapter Two

TOWARDS A MORE THEORY-BASED MEASUREMENT OF ORGANISATIONAL CLIMATE

P Conrad and J Sydow

Introduction

Organisational climate is considered to be a hypothetical construct of major managerial importance. It represents aggregate descriptions of organisational realities. The perceptual character of the construct implies the necessity of collecting data from the individual member of the organisation.

The purpose of this paper is to outline the methodological consequences of a perceptual approach to organisational climate, and to clarify the advantages and disadvantages of traditional approaches to the measurement of organisational climate. It will be demonstrated that these approaches are principally limited to grasping the aggregate and perceptual-cognitive character of the construct while, on the other hand, offering the well-known advantages of standardised questionnaires. The validity of those instruments seems to be doubtful when related to the theoretical concept of organisational climate. A standardised questionnaire is not able to grasp all those aspects of the organisational environment which potentially influence human behavior. Furthermore, questionnaires are typically not used to reveal the differential perspectives of the organisation's members as they mostly incorporate either the researcher's point of view or take a managerial perspective.

Organisational realities are subject to measurement by practitioners and social scientists. Managers, change agents, and scientists make use of institutional as well as of survey approaches to the measurement of organisational realities.

In most cases, both approaches are believed to represent alternative techniques. Organisational structure, for instance, is measured "objectively" as well as subjectively, that is "structure" is written about and is perceived by the organisation's members. Subjective measurement is assumed to be a convenient substitute for "objective" measurement. The methodological problems of survey measurement as a substitute for an institutional approach have often been overlooked, subjective data have seldom been validated against objective ones (Sathe, 1978). On the other hand, there are hypothetical constructs of organisational relevance such as work motivation, job satisfaction, and organisational climate which are perceptual in nature and hence cannot be measured using an institutional approach. However, in a phenomenological perspective, these constructs are as real as any "objective" structural property of an organisation.

Organisational climate as a hypothetical construct

For more than a decade, the concept of organisational climate has been subject to empirical investigation (e.g. Hellriegel and Slocum 1976, Joyce and Slocum 1979 and the studies by Paolillo 1982 and Abbey and Dickson 1983) and to intensive theoretical discussion (e.g. Gavin and Howe 1975, Schneider 1975, Payne et al. 1976, James et al. 1978, Powell and Butterfield 1978, Woodman and King 1978, Naylor et al. 1980, Field and Abelson 1982, Joyce and Slocum 1982, Schneider and Reichers 1983).

Climate is an "umbrella" term for various perceptual concepts which relate objective organisational properties to organisational behaviour, the latter being more a function of perceived rather than objective environments (Lewin, 1953). Organisational climate as a molar and global description of organisational realities is believed to influence a number of major issues of concern to those managing organisations such as:

- organisational performance through work motivation

- organisational absenteeism and turnover through job satisfaction

- organisational entry decisions through its attraction potential on new members.

Organisational climate is said to result from personal and situational factors such as motives, interests, cognitive complexity, leadership, organisational practices and policies. There is clearly a relationship between the concept of organisational climate, and organisational culture. However, the two terms are not synonymous.

If organisational culture is thought of as representing shared assumptions and values, it seems no large conceptual step from shared assumptions to shared perceptions. Culture can be conceptualised influencing climate in two aspects:

- directly, by establishing relevant cues for the evaluation for individual perceived organisational characteristics and procedures (Nauta 1984).

- indirectly, by partly shaping organisational "design philosophies" which in turn become manifest i.e. in the design of work organisations and thus are part of the directly perceivable organisational reality (Ashforth 1985).

The Powell and Butterfield (1978) review on organisational climate reveals that the following factors cause differences in climate perceptions:

1.   level of hierarchy
2.   line/staff position
3.   department/subunit
4.   biographical characteristics
5.   personality
6.   length of membership.

The significance of the climate construct to management practices rests on basically two assumptions:

-      that organisational climate influences organisational behaviour and hence organisational efficiency, and secondly

- that it can be managed by manipulating the situational characteristics of the organisation which interact with the personal characteristics of its members.

The unit of analysis in climate research is either the single organisational member (the psychological climate) or the organisation as a whole (the organisational climate). Besides psychological climate as a property of the individual member and organisational climate as a property of the whole organisation, climates of subunits, and climates of specific samples of people exist, but the only unit accessible for the measurement of climate is the single member of the organisation, since organisational climate is not directly observable. Yet no basis for aggregating individual data to organisational or subunit climates has been supported consistently on empirical grounds (Joyce and Slocum 1984).

The etiology of climates begins with the individual's perception of his or her work situation and of the wider organisational environment. Psychological climate is the individuals "cognitive representations that reflect on interpretation of the situation in terms that are psychologically meaningful to the individual (e.g. ambiguous, challenging, conflicting, cooperative, facilitative, fair, friendly, growth-oriented, supportive, trusting, warm)" (James et al. 1978, p. 785). Psychological climate becomes organisational climate when there is a significant consensus on climate perceptions.

Perceptual agreement on psychological climates may be termed "collective climates" (Joyce and Slocum 1984, p. 722).

The aggregate climate concept is useful in that it allows for descriptions of organisational settings in psychologically meaningful terms.

Since any consensus of climate perceptions is not necessarily caused by structural factors (e.g. departments) it may exist across organisational subunits. Johnston (1976), for example, identified a consensus on climate perceptions among newcomers as opposed to a climate for "old" members of an organisation. This has important implications for the management of the climate.

The following example illustrates the etiology of organisational climates on the collective level (see Figure 1 and Conrad and Sydow 1984.)

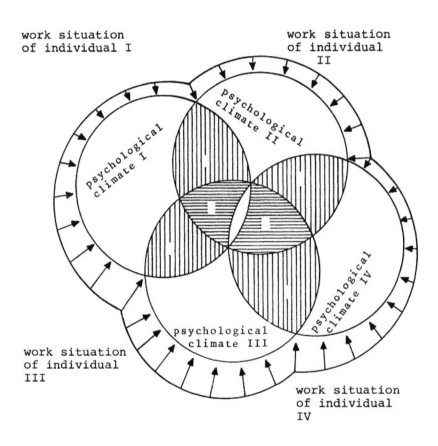

Figure 1: Work situations, psychological and
organisational climates

The organisation subjected to climate research consists of four members in work situations I - IV. From the perception of these work environments and from the cognitive processing of these data (e.g. abstraction, attribution) four distinct psychological climates emerge. In this case these climates partly overlap, hence creating seven organisational climates which can be traced back to:

1.   Individuals I and II use the same technology.

2.   Individuals II and IV entered the organisation five years ago.

3.   Individuals I and III carry out the same task.

4.   Individuals III and IV are characterised by an instrumental orientation towards work.

5.   Individuals I, II, III work in a group (group climate)

6.   Individuals II, III and IV stem from the same ethnic group.

7.   All four individuals are members of the same organisation (organisational climate in its narrow sense).

The general existence of organisational climate as an organisational property cannot be entirely specified by differences and similarities in situational and personal factors.   Those differences and similarities are caused by the socio-economic context which has an impact upon organisations as well as on its members. For instance, the capitalist mode of production is associated with particular organisational structures and causes structures to be fairly similar in terms of the distribution of authority and division of work. The   socio-economic   context   also   causes   the organisation's members to perceive the organisation in similar ways (see for example: Goldthorpe et al. 1968).   The process of socialisation in general and the   process   of   organisational   socialisation   in particular,   facilitates   the   emergence   of   similar cognitive   schemata   which   permit   individuals   to interpret their environment and to attribute meaning to it (Conrad and Sydow 1981).   This explanation of the etiology of organisational climate is supplemented by the attraction-selection theorem put forward by Schneider (Scheider and Reichers 1983).   However, the economic crisis reduces the value of this explanation of consensual perceptions because it is difficult for the individual to enter the organisation whose climate fits his or her expectations best.

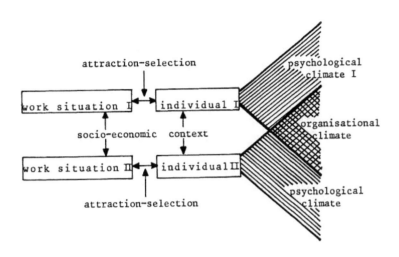

Figure 2: The etiology of consensual perceptions in organisations

The etiology of climate may be best understood from an interactional perspective (c.f. James et al. 1978, Schneider and Reichers 1983). The interactionist's position, according to Schneider and Reichers lies somewhere between objective and subjective approaches to organisation theory "based on the assumption that organisational reality is in part a social construction and that human beings are neither projectors nor responders, but rather actors and symbol users" (Schneider/Reichers 1983, p. 34). The interactional approach as used for the understanding of the etiology of climate emphasises reciprocal causation between the work situation, the individual (including his/her cognitive structures), and his/her behaviour (see Figure 3).

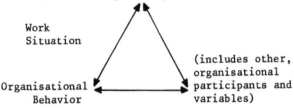

Figure 3: Interaction according to the social learning
theory of organisational behavour (Davis &
Luthans 1980, p. 283).

Interactionist thinking on organisational climate
blends "structuralist" or objectivist perspectives and
"attraction - selection" - or subjective approaches.
It claims understanding climate perceptions as results
of individual efforts, i.e. active cognitive
behaviour, in interpreting organisations and the roles
within them (Ashforth 1985).

The interactional approach which owes much to Lewinian
thought was first claimed to be an appropriate
framework for organisational analysis by Campbell et
al. (1970). Until recently, this approach has leant
on social learning theory as applied to organisational
behaviour (Davis and Luthans 1980). Related to the
etiology of organisational climates the interactional
framework of cognitive social learning theory implies
that:

1   Organisational behaviour results from situational
as well as from personal-cognitive factors (such as
organisation climate).

2   Behaviour may change situational factors but also
cognitive processing of climate-relevant information,
through learning for example, occurs.

3   Climate perceptions result from both the
individual's organisational behaviour as well as of
the behaviours of others.

4   The perception of situational factors is an
active process.

The organisational climate emerging from the
interaction of these variables bound together by their
common socio-economic context is multidimensional
(e.g. autonomy, structure, warmth, support) and

relatively stable over time. This stability implies that to change the organisational climate requires either management's stringent manipulation of one situational or personal factor, or a coordinated manipulation of several factors.

The following definition borrowing the term "hypothetical construct" from MacCorquodale and Meehl (1948) summarises the essential features of organisational climate:

"Organisational climate as a hypothetical construct is (1) a property of the whole organisation or one of its subunits, (2) a differentiating, (3) relatively stable, (4) molar and (5) multidivisional aggregate of subjective perceptions and cognitive processing of situational stimuli reflected by the individuals' description of the organisational context, structure and behaviour and influencing the formation of attitudes towards work and individual work behaviour" (Conrad and Sydow 1981, p. 3).

Organisational climate is almost always measured by standardised questionnaires from which the dimensions of the constructs are extracted using factor analysis techniques. When discussing the appropriateness of this traditional approach it has to be kept in mind that although this survey approach has been developed with earlier conceptualisations of organisational climate, it still is predominant even with the interactional approach.

Traditional approaches to the measurement of organisational climate

In total, almost a hundred empirical studies have been conducted on the relationship of organisational climate with some other organisational and/or personal variables (most of which are included in Hellriegel and Slocum 1976, Joyce and Slocum 1979, Conrad and Sydow 1984). In these studies one of about twenty standardised questionnaires have been used to measure the climate of schools, universities, business organisations and other institutions. Amongst the instruments available, the following have been most widely used:

Agency Climate Questionnaire (ACQ)
by Schneider and Bartlett (1970)
Business Organisation Climate Index (BOCI)
by Payne and Pheysey (1971)

Climate Index from the Survey of Organisations
by Taylor and Bowers (1972)
Climate Questionnaire (CQ)
by Litwin and Stringer (1968)
Group Dimension Description Questionnaire (GDDQ)
by Hemphill (1956)
Organisational Climate Description Questionnaire
(OCDQ) by Halpin and Croft (1962)
Organisational Climate Index (OCI)
by Stern (1970)
Psychological Climate Questionnaire (PCQ)
by Jones and James (1976)
Profile of Organisational Characteristics
by Likert (1967)

These questionnaires although fully standardised make use of rather different approaches to catch members' descriptions of the organisational environment. Consequently, these questionnaires do not only vary by the number of items but also by the character of the items (see Figure 4 for an example). While most of these questionnaires are omnibus measures and address themselves to the organisational climate as a whole, a few are restricted in their purpose and thus measure only a specific aspect of climate (leadership, industrial relations, safety etc.). Although a comprehensive compilation might be helpful, it is not the purpose of this paper to give an overview of all these instruments and to discuss them in detail. (One of the major problems is separating descriptive from evaluative items: see Schnake 1983). The following discussion will rather be restricted to the more fundamental problems of this approach to the measurement of organisational climate, namely from an interactional perspective.

> The jobs in this Organisation are clearly defined and logically structured.
> In this Organisation it is sometimes unclear who has the formal authority to make a decision.
> In this Organisation we set very high standards for performance.
> A friendly atmosphere prevails among the people in this Organisation.
> We don't rely too heavily on individual judgement in this Organisation; almost everything is double-checked.
> We are encouraged to speak our minds, even if it means disagreeing with our superiors.

The philosophy of our management is that in the long run we get ahead fastest by playing it slow, safe and sure.
People in this Organisation do not really trust each other enough.

Note: The subject could respond Definitely Agree, Inclined to Disagree, or Definitely Disagree.

Figure 4: Selected items from a climate questionnaire (Litwin and Stringer 1968)

Shortcomings of the traditional approaches

In most cases the purpose of measurement is to provide the data for statistical analyses. Their objective is to establish causal relationships. The following discussion will first focus on the traditional approaches used in climate research to establish these relationships. Then, the use of standardised questionnaires to measure organisational climate will be discussed.

The application of experimental research methods that seek to detect causal relationships is attempted where this will improve the clarity of results, where there is already an accumulated body of scientific knowledge, and where limitations of access to the research field itself dictate this approach. In this sense, experimental thought is employed.

If a relatively rigid definition of the experiment as a repeatable observation in a controlled situation, whereby one or more variables are manipulated in a manner that allows for the test of underlying hypotheses in different situations (Zimmerman 1972), is taken as standard, examples which reach this ideal are hard to find. One example is the climate study by Litwin and Stringer (1968). They tested members of three manipulated groups on relationships between leadership and group climate. The three groups consisted of members matched on several biographical dimensions which were considered to be influential on theoretical assumptions. By matching groups on the basis of several dimensions, one tries to eliminate suspected or known influences of other possible independent variables by establishing more or less identical conditions among the interrogated samples.

However, there are several weaknesses to this approach. Since the selected biographical dimensions were chosen on an a-priori basis and their intercorrelations are not presented in detail, it is difficult to estimate their overall scientific value since controlled factors tend to be intercorrelated (Selltitz et al. 1966) as it is not at all obvious which factors can be considered really influential. Internal validity of the results might be further reduced by the fact that a preselection of subjects has taken place (Litwin and Stringer 1968, p. 96). This could imply statistical regression (Campbell and Stanley 1966, Cook and Campbell 1976), and thus curtail the degree of variation in conceptually dependent variables. Furthermore, an experimental control group design had not been established; thus presumably the tested groups mutually functioned as control groups. Since statistical regression must be supposed because of preselected group members, the value of taking tested groups as control groups is further reduced. Though the Litwin and Stringer study could better be called a quasi-experiment it is one of the most thoroughly designed and the chosen experimental approach is very much recommended for further designs of climate studies.

The same arguments more or less also account for the Frederiksen, Jensen and Beaton study (1972) which also took place in a simulated organisation. This rigorously experimented study was designed to test the influence of different organisational climates on performance levels; several factor-analysed biographical and personal data were checked for moderating influences (c.f. Zedeck 1971). A sample of 260 male executives were randomly assigned to the several tested groups, but had not been randomly selected from their employing company. The random assignment to groups seems to be more appropriate than matching tested members on dimensions preselected on theoretical grounds, since it does not seem possible to evaluate influences on an a-priori basis, as long as the accumulated knowledge about organisational climate is rather unsystematic. Still a systematic selection of members from their employing organisations to become members of the simulated organisation would have been more appropriate, since selection effects (Frederiksen et al. 1972, p. 74) cannot be ruled out. Taking the studies together they demonstrate a clear proof of the appropriateness and feasibility of rigorous research practices on organisational climate; the achieved results are more likely to be considered a sound basis for further research than results from correlational analysis of data confounded with a wide array of uncontrolled variables.

Weaker designs than the above mentioned are the ex-post-facto arrangements. Here the concepts defined as independent represent past events whereas the conceptually dependent set of variables is measured in the present. Relationships between the two sets of variables are established ex-post with the identification of relationships based on correlational analyses (e.g. Johnston 1974, Payne and Mansfield 1973, Gavin 1975, Paolillo 1982). Normally, the complexity of the research setting in the social field automatically implies the unintended mix of independent variables with others (Cook and Campbell 1976). Thus the amounts of explained variance can be charged with alternative explanations. The Smircich and Chesser study (1981) for example investigated differential perceptions of 83 subordinates and 58 superiors in two organisations in respect of performance ratings. The supervisors had to rate their subordinates' performance (direct perspective) whereas the subordinates stated how they thought their supervisors would rate their performance (meta-perspective). The results showed strong differential perceptions between the two groups. The lack of similarity between the groups for example in respect to biographical dimensions like age, tenure, sex, etc. allows for no generalisations. Randomised selection of those questioned had not taken place. At best it could be called a "one shot case study" (Campbell and Stanley 1966) with nearly total absence of any statistical control. The scientific value must strongly be doubted. Plausibility arguments are added to justify the results, but they do not rest on scientific grounds. For example Smircich and Chesser from the disparity found in the perceptions draw the conclusion that the subordinates do not understand their superiors' perspectives. As this argument is based on correlational analysis and the applied techniques do not allow for causal inferences the reverse is equally true; i.e. the superiors do not understand their subordinates' role. In principal the same arguments also account for so-called multi-variate designs as long as manipulation of variables is only accomplished statistically.

Ansari, Baumgartel and Sullivan (1982) designed a study to test the hypothesis of statistical relationship (fit) between personal work orientation and organisational climate in determining career success among managers. Data were collected from 310 middle managers and 110 managers in 28 different company environments of British and American firms.

The applied analysis of variance is appropriate to identify statistically independent factors and thus to demonstrate relationships, but then they assume a random assignment of interrogated people to the several groups. Since this has not taken place the results must be strongly doubted and generalisations cannot be accepted. These doubts are supported by the lack of confirmation cross validating the achieved results on middle management level with top management employees in the same study. The fit hypothesis then must be considered invalid.

The value of ex post facto designs as a heuristic device is not questioned at all; however, their function in clarifying causal relationships in organisational research is doubtful, even if crosslag correlational analysis techniques are employed. Nonetheless, as Zimmerman (1972) points out, the large majority of research results in sociology is based on ex post facto designs. This seems to be equally true for the studies in organisational climate.

Field experiments allow studies in realistic settings; one variable or a set of independent variables must be manipulated and the situation in which the study takes place should be controlled most carefully. But less control takes place as compared with laboratory settings. A lower degree of control is combined with a higher degree of reality; reaction phenomena (experimenter biases, demand characteristics) are less likely to occur. If there is no manipulation of the independent factor, such a design could better be described as a field study (c.f. Kerlinger 1965, Friedrichs 1982). In this sense, field experiments could not be identified in our search.

Standardised questionnaire approaches

The existing instruments used in this kind of organisational climate research were constructed from the viewpoint of traditional test criteria (Lienert 1968); they vary not only by number and character of items and hence, factor-analysed dimensions but also by degree of mix between evaluative and non-evaluative items and scale properties.

As far as factor-analytic techniques were applied in statistically determining relevant climate dimensions, different break-off criteria and methods of factor rotation were used. Additionally variations in the factor loadings of items, in the number of extracted factors and their factorial interdependence lead to the extraordinary decrease in comparability (Schneider and Hall 1972, Gavin and Howe 1975, Herman et al. 1975, Maynard 1974, Waters et al. 1974, Offenberg and Cernius 1978).

A rather elaborate way to improve existing knowledge about organisational climate is to validate existing instruments against each other or against any theoretically based external criterion. Validity studies of this kind should be based on instruments fulfilling conventional measurement - criteria. Those studies are rare and the validity-of-the-criterion problem is still unsolved (Ansari et al. 1982, Rosenstiel et al. 1982). Instead, empirical studies aim at statistically significant results. But Mintzberg (1979) is right in asking, "Was it better to have less valid data that were statistically significant?" (p. 583) and in proposing more direct methodologies that produce significant results not only in the statistical sense of the word. Indeed, the more standardised the instruments are, the less valid they may be (Berger 1980, p. 26 f.).

The survey approach in general only seems adequate when certain test-quality standards (like objectivity, reliability and validity) are met. Normally the usage of these instruments is not limited to any specific organisation; they can therefore be applied to different organisations and produce a huge amount of computable information once constructed. Thus, at first glance, this seems to be a convenient and reasonable method of data collection.

However several deficiencies are inherent in the application of such instruments, specifically in organisational climate studies. The arguments against the application of standardised instruments are mostly theoretical and less statistical.

First of all a sound solution for the unit of analysis problem seems to be out of sight. The unit of data collection in these instruments is the single organisational member, whereas the group, department, or level in the hierarchy or the organisation as a whole is used in the results. Aggregation problems are only solved statistically by averaging individual scores, but not on any explicitly stated statistical models or theoretical grounds (c.f James 1982). "There is also a need to establish some consensus about the criteria for accepting aggregate statistics as valid indicators of a social collectivity ... Even if such a consensus is impossible to establish it is important that future research looks at more than just the mean as a description of any social collectivity" (Payne et al. 1976, p. 59).

A second problem area is the adequate construction of the "item pool". Standardised questionnaires are usually developed by researchers (or partly by organisational practitioners) and most likely reflect their point of view. Their beliefs about organisational realities and their judgements about the relevance of single aspects or dimensions of organisational climate are implicitly implemented in the construction process. This prefabrication of survey stimuli and the assignment of distinct scale properties restricts the variety of possible answers to very few.

The idiosyncratic relevance of these items to the survey participants is not at all proven. Instead the questionnaires tend to press verbal responses of organisational members into categories which may not be appropriate in the view of those who were questioned. Hence, the representativeness of these categories should be a matter for investigation.

Instead of taking organisational members as actors and symbol users, as epistemic subjects (Groeben and Scheele 1977; Ashforth 1985) organisational members are reduced to response emitting organisms. This is even true for questionnaires which have been developed most carefully and have overcome some of the obstacles of more conventional instruments (e.g. Rosenstiel et al. 1982). The common nomothetic approach underlying quantitative measurement tends to average individual response scores and thus eliminates the dissimilarities of individuals found in reality as well as excluding person-situation interactions (Reichardt and Cook 1979, Luthans and Davis 1982). To us differential perceptions among organisational members are "... not a methodological distress but a constituent part of organisational reality" (Kubicek et al. 1981, p. 101). Organisational climate is a facet of subjectively interpreted reality, interpreted by those, who were themselves part of that reality.

In all, traditional research instruments risk the production of artifacts, i.e. organisational climate as the product of loosely sampled items and of the methodology used. Artifacts can result from inappropriate measurement as well as from inadequate statistical analysis (Kriz 1981). Thus an established organisational climate is not necessarily bound to organisational reality or its reconstruction in the minds of organisational members. Organisational members "enact" their environments (Weick 1979 b). It therefore seems likely that research outputs tend to picture only small facets of existing climates, dispelling the phenomenal and molar character (see Figure 5). At worst, organisational climate turns out to be a method-bound concept.

In summary we can state that:

- causal relationships in climate research could not be identified up to the present

- important theoretical features of the concept are not adequately caught by traditional approaches.

We therefore suggest a more idiographic approach at least at the very beginning of the research process and to leave standardised measurement to the time when more knowledge has been accumulated systematically.

A more idiographic approach does not imply that social structures and regularities in organisations are assumed to be non-existent. On the contrary, it has been argued that these structures and their cognitive mediation through socialisation contribute significantly to the etiology of organisational climate. The critical statement made by Kubicek, Woolnik and Kieser (1981, p. 90) seems convincing: "Universalism, inherent to standardised measurement techniques precedes the clarification of the theoretical foundation of a general organisation theory".

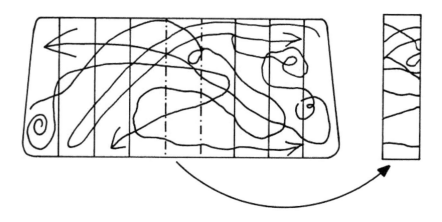

Figure 5: Slicing up to the organisation by means of
traditional methodologies
(Mintzberg 1979, p. 585)

The interactional approach to organisational climate,
in our view, means qualitative measurement, at least
to begin with. We think that the application of
standardised instruments in organisational climate
research is inappropriate and that existing
instruments concentrate too much on test-quality
standards, instead of identifying basic differential
interpretations of organisational reality.

Towards an improved measurement of organisational
climate

The methodological shortcomings of traditional climate
research are not surprising since most of these
instruments have not been derived from a thorough
theory of organisational climate. This is
particularly true as the theory of organisational
climate itself had neglected individual differences
and their effects on climate perceptions for quite a
long period of time. At the time of the development
of most climate questionnaires, the concept was still
lacking its theoretical foundation in interactional

psychology and social learning theory. Morgan and Smircich (1980) summarise the subjectivity - objectivity debate within social sciences in Figure 6.

The position of organisational climate, according to the interactional approach outlined above, would be in the middle of the chart pointing to symbolic analysis and hermeneutics as the appropriate research method. Thus, an appropriate method for climate research lies somewhere between the extremes of organisational inquiry, namely the "inquiry from the inside" and the "inquiry from the outside", the one "being methodologically precise, but often irrelevant to the reality of organisations, the other (being) crucially relevant, but often too vague to be communicated to or believed by others" (Evered and Louis 1981, p. 392; see also Campbell 1979).

One potentially relevant technique is the qualitative interview (also termed narrative interview, focussed interview, clinical interview or clinical interrogation) which is probably best known and controversial (cf. Kubicek 1975, Kohli 1978, Friedrichs 1982, Osterloh 1982). Qualitative interviews aim at the actualisation of everyday experience in order to gather valid data without externally structuring the interviewer's perspective. In contrast to techniques which may be subsumed under the "inquiry from the inside" the qualitative interviewer has a chance of being aware of the methodological problems associated with interviews in organisational settings (cf. Osterloh 1982). Notwithstanding the difficulty in establishing validity aspects and the lack of direct comparability among questioned persons, it seems to offer several advantages, when properly applied and not taken mainly as a testing device. By contrast, standardised and structured instruments tend to be based on the stimulus material produced by the researcher, as well as the questioned population.

The general proposal to make more use of qualitative measurement approaches at least in the conceptualisation stages of the research process does not mean at all that the measurement and the application of several statistical methods should be abandoned. The interpretive character of social relationships requires qualitative methods which emphasise communications with organisational members rather than standardised questionnaires. However, the former is not necessarily a substitute for quantitative analysis in general. Qualitative data may be subject to statistical analysis (Hopf 1979), but, the emphasis is on an exact description of social reality, i.e. the organisational climate.

When organisational members describe their organisational realities the interview data contain different concepts. Three classes of concepts can be distinguished (cf. Kromrey 1980):

- metrical concepts (like length, income)

- rank ordering concepts (like bigger, better, friendlier etc.)

- classification concepts (like department, kind of task)

The concepts and their individual interrelation can be thought of as establishing a personal network of descriptive elements to picture organisational realities.

By the application of an appropriate statistical model the individually used concepts can be submitted to statistical analysis on an individual and a group basis. Concepts and networks of concepts serve as individually relevant anchor points in climate perception and can be taken as starting points for developing instruments which systematically include the organisational members' frames of references. Thereby differential perspectives of different organisational members can be integrated and the obstacles of one-sided views in measurement can be partly overcome.

Only very recently have quantitative tools been used which avoid simply "adding" individual climate scores or averaging established collective climates. The identification of profile similarities on several climate dimensions and their clustering seem to be relevant research approaches, allowing for the empirical demonstration of patterns of individual perceptual processing.

The empirically based construction of such patterns, their comparison and aggregation seem to be successful ways of reconciling the different perspectives of organisational members and thus overcoming measurement problems in the organisational climate approach. (Joyce and Slocum 1984).

Qualitative instruments start off from a more conceptual level and probably allow for a better identification of different concepts constituting climate perceptions. In a so called "iterative process" (Kubicek 1977) the researcher's preconceptions, loosely combined into a manual are confronted with the ideas, problems and needs of the interrogated sample. In principle this process, mostly arranged as a two or more person interaction, allows for:

- the achievement of information concerning specific aspects and needs of the questioned persons

- the enlargement of response possibilities

- an elaboration of idiosyncratic positions

- the investigation into personal frames of reference, which serve as the basis for organisationally relevant judgements by organisation members (Weick 1979 a)

The process of concept development is systematically fed back, ensuring a broader and more appropriate data basis. Obviously the process could be endless, if one did not define any kind of satisfactory limit to it. A quantitative solution to this problem could be the representative selection of individuals to be interrogated in the organisation under investigation. The gathered data can then be analysed by means of quantitative methods. Classification concepts, rank-order concepts and metrical concepts might serve as anchor points to extract individually relevant climate concepts. In a further step interpersonal relevant climate dimensions can be established on the basis of individual ones plus a statistically defined similarity index. Once this has been established the more traditional correlational or experimental approaches should be applied.

In summary an approach based on qualitative techniques should provide a sound basis for the reconstruction of processes applied by organisation members to describe their environments. Our intention is not to argue that standardised questionnaires should be abandoned from climate research or to claim that all empirical findings are invalid. However, we do propose a critical attitude towards the exclusive use of these traditional approaches to the measurement of organisational climate. A thorough research on alternative methodologies of climate research is urgently needed. This research might end up with the recommendation of:

(1) a pluralistic, multi-method approach to the measurement of organisational climate making use of competitive research designs,

(2) better, that is more theory-based questionnaires, or

(3) a blend of qualitative methods. This combination is also called "triangulation". The notion of triangulation is not restricted to "within-methods" strategies. Triangulation " ... can also capture a more complete, holistic, and contextual portrayal of the unit(s) under study. That is beyond the analysis of overlapping variance, the use of multiple measures may uncover some unique variance which otherwise may have been neglected by single methods. It is here that qualitative methods, in particular, can play an especially prominent role by eliciting data and suggesting conclusions to which other methods would be blind. ..." "In this sense, triangulation may be used not only to examine the same phenomenon from multiple perspectives but also to enrich our understanding by allowing for new or deeper dimensions to emerge" (Jick 1979, p. 603-604). Finally the superiority of one of these three approaches to the measurement of organisational climate would have to be established.

Figure 6: Elements of Subjective and Objective Approaches

	Subjectivist Approaches to Social Science					Objectivist Approaches to Social Science
Core Ontological Assumptions	reality as a projection of human imagination	reality as a social construction	reality as a realm of symbolic discourse	reality as a contextual field of information	reality as a concrete process	reality as a concrete structure
Assumptions About Human Nature	man as pure spirit consciousness, being	man as a social constructor, the symbol creator	man as an actor the symbol user	man as an information processor	man as an adaptor	man as a responder
Basic Epistemological Stance	to obtain phenomenological insight, revelation	to understand how social reality is created	to understand patterns of symbolic discourse	to map contexts	to study systems, process, change	to construct a positivist science
Some favoured Metaphors	transcendental	language game, accomplishment, text	theatre, culture	cybernetic	organism	machine
Research Methods	exploration of pure subjectivity	hermeneutics	symbolic analysis	contextual analysis of Gestalten	historical analysis	lab experiments, surveys

References

Abbey, A and Dickson, J W (1983): R & D work climate and innovation in semiconductors. In: Academy of Management Journal, 26(2), 362-368.

Ansari, N A, Baumgartel, H and Sullivan, G (1982): The personal orientation - organisational climate fit and managerial success. In: Human Relations, 35, 1159-1178.

Ashforth, B E (1985) Climate formation: issues and extensions. In: Academy of Management Review 10(4), 837-847.

Berger, H (1980): Untersuchungsmethode und soziale Wirklichkeit. Frankfurt.

Campbell, D T: "Degrees of freedom" and the case study. In: Cook, T D and Reichardt, C S (eds.): Qualitative and quantitative methods in evaluation research, pp. 49-67, Beverly Hills u. London.

Campbell, D T and Stanley, J C (1966): Experimental and quasi-experimental designs for research. Chicago.

Campbell, J P, Dunnette, M D and Lawler, E E III and Weick, K E Jr. (1970): Managerial behaviour, performance, and effectiveness. New York.

Conrad, P and Sydow, J (1981): Die Formulierung des Organisationsklimas als hypothetisches Konstrukt. Working paper No. 40/81 of the Institute of Management, Freie Universität Berlin.

Conrad, P and Sydow, J (1984) Organisationsklima. Berlin and New York.

Cook, T D and Campbell, D T (1976): The design and conduct of quasi-experiments and true experiments in field settings. In: Dunnette, M D (ed.): Handbook of industrial and organisational psychology, 223-326. Chicago.

Davis, T R V and Luthans, F (1980): A social learning approach to organisational behaviour. In: Academy of Management Review, 5(2), 281-290.

Evered, R and Louis, M R (1981): Alternative
    perspectives in the organisational sciences:
    "Inquiry from the inside" and "Inquiry from the
    outside". In: Academy of Management Review, 6(3),
    385-395.

Field, R H G and Abelson, M A (1982): Climate: A
    reconceptualisation and proposed model. In: Human
    Relations, 35(3), 181-201.

Frederiksen, N, Jensen, O and Beaton, A E (1972):
    Prediction of organisational behaviour. New York
    etc.

Friedrichs, J (1982): Methoden empirischer
    Sozialforschung. Opladen.

Gavin, J F (1975): Organisational climate as a
    function of personal and organisational variables.
    In: Journal of Applied Psychology, 60, 135-139.

Goldthorpe, J H, Lockwood, D L, Bechefer, F and Platt,
    J (1968): The affluent worker. Cambridge.

Groeben, N and Scheele, B (1977): Argumente fur eine
    Psychologie des reflexiven Subjektes. Darmstadt.

Halpin, A W and Croft, D P (1962): The organisational
    climate of schools. Research Report No. CRP-543.
    US Department of Health, Education and Welfare.

Hellriegel, D and Slocum, J W Jr. (1974):
    Organisational climate: Measures, research, and
    contingencies. In: Academy of Management Journal,
    17(2), 255-280.

Hemphill, J K (1956): Group dimensions. A manual for
    their measurement. Research Monograph No. 87.
    Bureau of Business Research. Ohio State
    University.

Herman, J B, Dunham, R B and Hulin, C L (1975):
    Organisational structure, demographic
    characteristics, and employee responses. In:
    Organisational Behaviour and Human Performance,
    13, 206-232.

Hopf, Ch (1979). Soziologie und qualitative
    Sozialforschung. In: Hopf, Ch. and Weingarten, E
    (Hrsg.): Qualitative Sozialforschung. Stuttgart,
    11-37.

James, L R (1982): Aggregation bias in estimates of perceptual agreement. In: Journal of Applied Psychology, 67(2), 219-229.

James, L R, Hater, J J, Gent, M J and Bruni, J R (1978): Psychological climate: implications from cognitive social learning theory and interactional psychology. In: Personnel Psychology, 31, 783-813.

Jick, T D (1979): Mixing qualitative and quantitative methods: Triangulation in action. In: Administrative Science Quarterly, 24, 602-611.

Johnston, H R (1976): A new conceptualisation of sources of organisational climate. In: Administrative Science Quarterly, 21(1), 95-103.

Jones, A P and James, L R (1976): Psychological and organisational climate: dimensions and relationships. Techn. Rep. 76-4. Institute of Behavioural Research. Texas Christian University. Forth Worth, Texas.

Joyce, W F and Slocum, J W Jr. (1979): Climates in organisations. In: Kerr, St. (Ed.): Organisational behaviour. Columbus, Ohio, 317-333.

Joyce, W F and Slocum, J (1982): Climate discrepancy: Refining the concepts of psychological and organisational climate. In: Human Relations, 35(11), 951-972.

Joyce, W F and Slocum, J W (1984) Collective climate. Agreement as a basis for defining aggregate climates in organisations. In: Academy of Management Journal 27(4): 721-742

Kerlinger, F N (1965): Foundations of behavioural research. New York.

Kohli, M (1978): "Offenes" und "geschlossenes" Interview: Neue Argumente zu einer alten Kontroverse. In: Soziale Welt, 29, 1-25.

Kriz, J (1981): Methodenkritik empirischer Sozialforschung. Eine Problemanalyse sozialwissenschaftlicher Forschungspraxis. Stuttgart.

Kromrey, H (1980): Empirische Sozialforschung. Oplanden.

Kubicek, H (1975): Empirische Organisationsforschung. Stuttgart.

Kubicek, H (1977): Heuristische Bezugsrahmen und heuristisch angelegte Forschungsdesigns als Elemente einer Konstruktionsstrategie empirischer Forschung. In: Kohler, R (Hrsg.): Empirische und handlungstheoretische Forschungskonzeptionen in der Betriebswirtschaftslehre. Stuttgart, 3-36.

Kubicek, H, Wollnik, M and Kieser, A. (1981): Wege zur praxisorientierten Erfassung der formalen Organisationsstruktur. In: Witte, E (Hrsg.): Der praktische Nutzen empirischer Forschung. Tubigen, 79-114.

Lewin, K (1951): Field theory and social science. New York.

Lienert, G A (1969): Testaufbau und Testanalyse. Weinheim etc.

Likert, R (1967): The human organisation. New York etc.

Litwin, G H and Stringer, R A, Jr. (1968): Motivation and organisational climate. Boston.

Luthans, F and Davis, T R V (1982): An idiographic approach to organisational behaviour research: The use of single case experimental designs and direct measurement. In: Academy of Management Review, 7(3), 380-391.

MacCorquodale, K and Meehl, P E (1948): On a distinction between hypothetical constructs and intervening variables. In: Psychological Review, 55, 95-107.

Maynard, W J, Jr. (1974): Organisational and individual correlates of organisational climate perceptions. Dissertation. Ann Arbor, Mich.

Mintzberg, H (1979): An emerging strategy of "direct" research. In: Administrative Science Quarterly, 24, 582-589.

Morgan, G and Smircich, L (1980): The Case for
Qualitative Research. In: Academy of Management
Review, 5, 491-500.

Nauta, R (1984) Climate and culture. In: Koopman-
Iwema, A.M. and Roe, R A (eds): Work and
organisational psychology, European perspectives,
255-275

Naylor, J C, Pritchard, R D and Ilgen, D R (1980): A
theory of behaviour in organisations. New York
etc.

Offenberg, R M and Cernius, V (1978): Assessment of
idiographic organisational climate. In: Journal
of Applied Behavioural Science, 14, 79-86.

Osterloh, M (1982): Pladoyer für eine breitere
Anwendung qualitätiver Interviews in der
empirischen Organisationsforschung. Working paper
No. 41'82 of the Institute of Management. Freie
Universität Berlin.

Paolillo   J G P (1982): R&D subsystem climate as a
function of personal and organisational factors.
In: Journal of Management Studies, 19(3), 327-334.

Payne, R L and Pheysey, D C (1971): Stern's
organisational climate index: a
reconceptualisation and application to business
organisations. In: Organisational Behaviour and
Human Performance, 6, 77-98. Reprinted in: Pugh,
D S and Payne, R L (1977) (eds.): Organisational
behaviour in its context. The Aston programme
III. Saxon House. Westmead, Hants, 113-133.

Payne, R L and Mansfield, R (1973): Relationships of
perceptions of organisational climate to
organisational structure, context, and
hierarchical position. In: Administrative Science
Quarterly, 18, 515-526.

Payne, R L, Fineman, S and Wall, T D (1976):
Organisational climate and job satisfaction: a
conceptual synthesis. In: Organisational
Behaviour and Human Performance, 16, 45-62.

Powell, G N and Butterfield, D A (1978): The case
for subsystem climates in organisations. In:
Academy of Management Review, 3, 151-157.

Reichardt, C J and Cook, T D (1979): Beyond qualitative versus quantitative methods. In: Cook, T D and Reichardt, C J (Eds.): Qualitative and quantitative methods in evaluation research, 7-32. Beverly Hills London.

Rosenstiel, L V, Falkenberg, Th, Henn, W, Henschel, E and Warns, I (1982): Betriebsklima heute. Forschungsbericht im Auftrag des Bayerischen Staatsministeriums für Arbeit und Sozialordnung, München.

Sathe, V (1978): Institutional versus questionnaire measures of organisational structure. In: Academy of Management Journal, 21, 227-238.

Schnake, M E (1983) An empirical assessment of the effects of affective response in the measurement of organisational climate. In: Personnel Psychology 36(3):791-807.

Schneider, B (1975): Organisational climates: an essay. In: Personnel Psychology, 28, 447-479.

Schneider, B and Barlett, C J (1970): Individual differences and organisational climate II: Measurement of organisational climate as the multi-trait, multi-rater matrix. In: Personnel Psychology, 23, 493-512.

Schneider, B and Hall, D T (1972): Toward specifying the concept of work climate: A study of Roman Catholic Diocesan priests. In: Journal of Applied Psychology, 56, 447-455.

Schneider, B and Reichers, A E (1983): On the etiology of climates. In: Personnel Psychology, 36, 19-39.

Selltitz, C, Jahoda, M, Deutsch, M and Cook, St W (1966): Research methods in social relations. New York.

Smircich, L and Chesser, R J (1981): Superiors' and subordinates' perceptions of performance: Beyond disagreement. In: Academy of Management Journal, 24, 198-205.

Stern, G C (1970): People in context: measuring person-environment congruence in education and industry. New York.

Taylor, J C and Bowers, D G (1972): Survey of
    Organisations. A maschine-scored standardised
    questionnaire instrument. Ann Arbor, Michigan.

Waters, L K, Roach, D and Batlis, N (1974):
    Organisational climate dimensions and job-related
    attitudes. In: Personnel Psychology, 27, 465-476.

Weick, K E (1979a): Cognitive processes in
    organisations. In: Staw, B M (ed.): Research in
    Organisational behaviour, vol. 1, Greenwich,
    Conn., 41-74.

Weick, K E (1979b). The social psychology of
    organising. 2nd ed. Reading, Mass.

Woodman, R E and King, D C (1978): Organisational
    climate: science or folklore? In: Academy of
    Management Review, 3, 816-826.

Zedeck, Sh (1971): Problems with the use of
    "moderator" variables. In: Psychological
    Bulletin, 295-310.

Zimmerman, E (1972): Das Experiment in den
    Sozialwissenschaften. Stuttgart.

Chapter Three

ORGANISATIONAL CLIMATE: A PROVISIONAL MODEL FOR ORGANISATIONAL EFFECTIVITY

G De Cock, R Bouwen, K De Witte and J De Visch

Organisational climate has been the focus of study for several years. We consider organisational climate as a general notion specifying the organisational identity or self image of the organisation: e.g. how members see their organisation work, live, decide, reward, grow.

We agree with the conclusions of Srivasta et al (1975) and Steers (1977) who argue that the organisational climate affects the behaviour of the members of the organisation. We summarised this in the following scheme (De Witte, 1985).

Figure 1   Organisational Climate Model (De Witte, 1985)

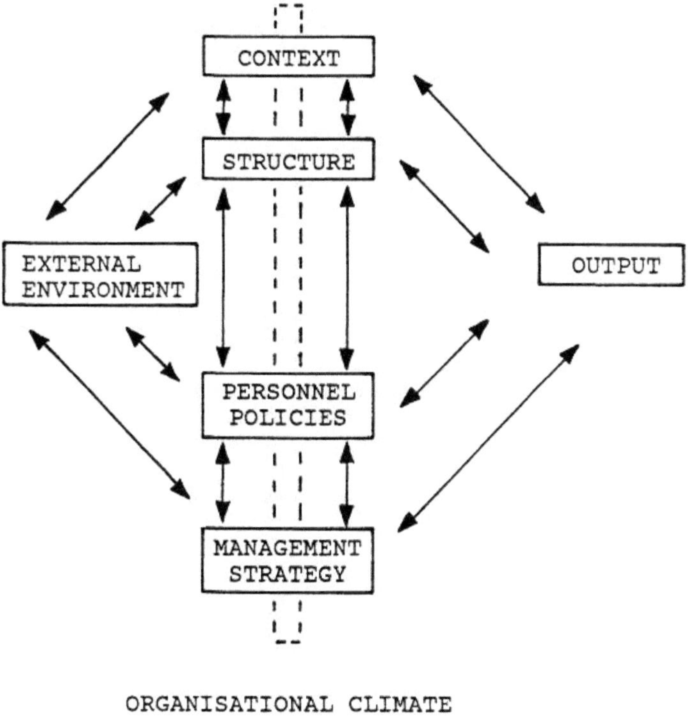

ORGANISATIONAL CLIMATE

45

We started the project with the construction of a Dutch organisational climate instrument. We used the Business Organisational Climate Index (Payne and Mansfield, 1973) as an immediate source to develop the instrument. This index originated as a psychological framework for understanding how the environment was conceptualised.

We translated the items and added new items. The questionnaire now contains 202 items, distributed over 20 scales. We named this instrument the OK1PO (De Cock and De Witte, 1978). This instrument was used to investigate the relations between organisational climate and organisational variables such as size, formalisation of role definition, functional specialisation and personal variables such as position in hierarchy, age and seniority. We see the Leuven study as an extension of the Aston study.

At the same time a project was started to study the organisational climate in hospitals and we developed an organisational climate instrument for this. Using factor analysis, two dimensions appeared after orthogonal rotation. The first dimension related to stabilising elements in the organisation for example, control by superiors, structure and role orientation. The second dimension included dynamic elements in the organisation such as socio-emotional relations, readiness to innovate, goal orientation and reward orientation. These two factors closely resemble those of Stern (1970). He found two second-order factors when factor analysing the Organisational Climate Index: 1. Growth and self-enhancement; 2. Stability and self-maintenance. Payne and Pheysey (1971) also mentioned two factors when factor analysing the Business Organisational Climate Index: organisational progressiveness; and normative control. Those two dimensions functioned as a starting-point to construct the organisational climate instruments for hospitals. After item-analysis, the total questionnaire contained 27 items, distributed over two scales.

Two reasons prompted us to reconstruct the OKIPO. First a theoretically based instrument is more useful than an instrument where detached scales are used. When scales can be connected with a number of views about organisational functioning, it allows us to make some assumptions on the factors influencing the organisational climate. In this connection, our research findings on hospitals resembled a more elaborated climate reference scheme described by Quinn (1983) which has been successfully applied on organisational climate (De Visch, 1983). Secondly, using a short instrument meant a considerable cost saving for the organisation, and organisational members were motivated to fill in such a questionnaire.

In this chapter we will deal initially with the reference scheme and construction of the short organisational climate instrument for profit organisations. At a further point an integration of literature and research findings allows us to develop a provisional model for organisational effectiveness.

The competing values framework

Quinn (1983) noticed that organisational researchers and managers ask three questions when comparing organisations. Firstly, does the organisation emphasise the growth of the people in or the goals of the organisation? On the one hand members of the organisation have a unique set of feelings and wishes. On the other hand the organisation exists to reach certain goals and to carry out tasks. A manager can pay attention to both aspects in the organisation, although one aspect is mostly emphasised. We place this first polarity on the horizontal axis in Figure two below.

Secondly, is the organisation flexible with regard to the environment or aimed at controlling the existing situation? Certain organisations emphasise authority, structure and coordination, others emphasise diversity, individual initiative and adaptation to the environment. We place this second polarity on the vertical axis in Figure two.

MODEL FOR ORGANISATIONAL EFFECTIVITY

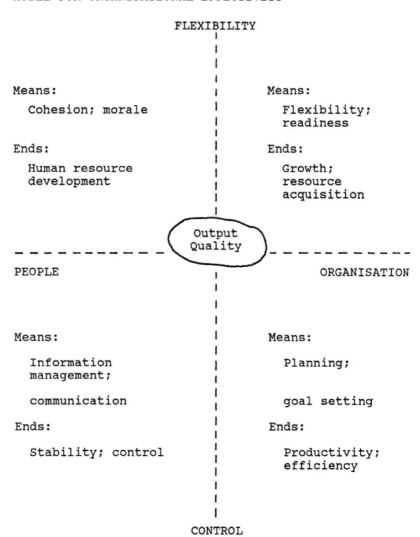

Figure 2: A simplified model of the competing values
scheme. (Based on Quinn and Rohrbaugh,
1983, p.369)

Both questions appear as dilemmas. In his career the manager makes choices and decisions through which the organisation evolves in a certain direction, for example he can give the R and D centre in his organisation more autonomy. This decision can let the organisation evolve more flexibility.

At the Centre for Organisational and Personnel Psychology the results of research in hospitals, together with the competing values framework, functioned as a direct source to construct an abridged organisational climate instrument for profit organisations. We operationalised each field in the competing values framework. Organisational experts selected from the OKIPO items which could be placed in one quadrant of the framework only. It was self-evident the items also had to discriminate between organisations. We obtained this discrimination index through a one way variance over 28 organisations. Those items were held back which differentiated on the 0.001 significance level between organisations.

Factor analysis was used to test the grouping of items. Items which belonged to two or more factors were eliminated. After an iterative item analysis the questionnaire contained 39 items, distributed over four scales. We gave those scales the following names: support, innovation, respect for rules and goal oriented information flow (see Figure 3). The reliability of the scales is shown in Table 1. The validity has been tested by factor analysis of another group of organisations.

We placed the first scale, "support", top left in Figure 3. It relates to the opinions of organisational members with regard to each other and with regard to their superiors. The results on this scale indicated how organisational members trust, help and respect each other. Top right in the competing values scheme we place the "innovation" scale. The essential point here is the extent to which members perceive a tendency for improvement in the organisation. This includes studying after work hours, showing a broad interest, showing creativity and taking scientific investigations and changing factors in the environment into account.

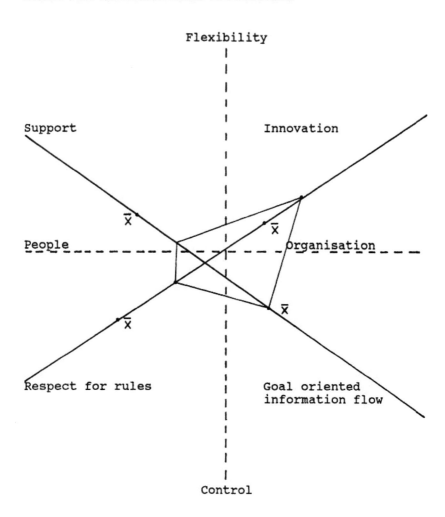

Figure 3: An application of the competing values
scheme on organisational climate.

Bottom left in Figure 3 is the scale "respect for rules". The responses indicate how organisational members experience a strict description of their work and control on the quality and quantity of their work. Bottom right we place the scale "goal oriented information flow." This indicates how the members experience clarity in their tasks and the coordination between their tasks.

Four aggregate scores, one for each scale, can be determined for an organisation. Integrating these results allows the diagnostician to make a pictorial representation of the organisational climate (as in Figure 3).

Visualising the aggregate scores of the organisational climate instrument makes the interpretation easier. For example, let us take the case of the organisation represented in Figure 3. This organisation scores high on innovation, moderate on goal oriented information flow and low on support and respect for rules. These scores refer to an organisational climate characterised by a strong tendency for improvement and change. Deviation from existing regulations is perceived as possible. In addition to this, members also experience clarity in their tasks. However the organisation scores low on the support scale. This could refer to a certain rivalry between the members of the organisation. A lack of cooperation could hinder high innovativeness. Suppose the organisation had a high score on the support scale? Then we could argue that high innovativeness is impeded because people feel too free.

As a matter of course, those interpretations are more penetrating when scale scores can be connected with a theoretical framework in which the factors influencing organisational climate are more elaborated.

A provisional model for organisational effectiveness

The competing values framework renders it possible to make some assumptions on the factors that influence the organisational climate. When we know how the organisational climate is influenced, we can get indications about how to change it.

To get an overall picture of the possible factors that influence organisational climate we can refer to several models organisational experts and investigators have developed. We can conceive each theory as a way a researcher looks at the complexity of an organisation. Each vision is a way to approach organisational reality. Four common models are the human relations, the open systems, the internal process and the rational goal models. It is also possible to place the four organisational cultures of Handy (1981) and Harrison (1972) in the competing values framework. These authors describe four organisational cultures, namely directed on persons, power, roles and tasks. We place these cultures in Figure 4 and we describe the four organisational types. An investigation has demonstrated the usefulness and realistic value of the underlying theory and the instrument (De Witte, 1985).

Top left we place person-oriented organisations. In this culture the person is the central point. Values, opinions and emotions of organisational members play an important role. Informal structures dominate. This was emphasised in the human-relations model. Person-oriented organisations exist only to serve and assist the individuals within them. There are no global objectives which transcend individual objectives. Alcoholics Anonymous clubs and communes are examples of such organisations. Naturally there is as little structure as possible. Handy (1981) represents this organisation by a cluster, a little structured collection of individuals, where social contact is highly valued by each of them. Such an organisation corresponds closely to Ouchi's "Theory Z organisation" or clan. Human involvement forms the central point. Decisions are made in an informal manner. The leadership style is personal and relation oriented. These organisational characteristics stimulate a supportive organisational climate.

Top right we place the open systems model and task oriented organisation. In the open systems model events in the organisation cannot be explained by internal variables only. There is a fundamental interdependence between elements in the organisation and between the organisation and its environment. Change in one element leads to changes in other elements. Therefore continuous adaptation is necessary. Such a flexibility is necessary to reach organisational goals. According to Handy, the structure of this organisation resembles that of a net. Some wires are stronger than others, power is concentrated on the intersections. An example is the modern matrix organisation.

Flexibility

cluster

Person oriented
culture

Human relations model

net

Task oriented
culture

Open system model

People ———————————————————————— Organisation

Internal
process-model

Role oriented
culture

 temple

Rational goal
model

Power oriented
culture

web

Control

Figure 4: An integration of four approaches of
organisation theories in the competing
values framework.

Authority is accepted if it is based on knowledge and
skill. Rules may be infringed, if it can be shown
that it is important to complete the task. Control is
restricted to a minimum. These organisations work in
complex and changing environments, in dynamic markets.
Flexibility and sensitivity to the market or
environment are important. Therefore teams are formed
around specific problems, products or services. The
team members work together on the basis of equality.
Conflicts are solved by mutual arrangements. They
are seen by the organisational members as
opportunities to learn. Mintzberg (1981) called this
organisation an adhocracy. The organisational climate
is highly innovative.

Opposite the task oriented organisation we can place a role oriented organisation. The role structure is, according to Handy, characterised by a centralised structure and a formalised system of rules and procedures. Equilibrium is the central point of interest. Conflict and tensions are kept at a minimum. Academics called this model the internal process model. This organisation is characterised by procedures for roles, procedures for communications and rules for the settlement of disputes. Order and systems form the central point of interest. The accompanying structure works by logic and by rationality. The role organisation has its strength in its pillars, its functions or specialities. The work of the pillars, and the interaction between the pillars is controlled by a narrow band of senior management, the roof of the temple. Stability and rationality of the allocation of work are more important than capacity. Ouchi (1980) describes this organisation as a hierarchy. The characteristics of this organisation are procedures and the organisational climate is characterised by respect for rules.

In the last section, bottom right, we place the rational model and the power oriented organisation. In a power oriented culture the optimal use of resources and the making of priorities are important. This culture often depends on a central power source. Power oriented organisations can best be pictured like a web, with rays of power and influence spreading from the central figure. It is important to anticipate the wishes and decisions of that central power source. These organisations have the ability to move quickly and can react well to threat or danger. When circumstances are hazardous and there is much competitition the organisation reacts aggressively. The person in the middle plays a crucial role. If the spider moves, the whole web trembles. The validity of the decision depends strongly on the capacity of the spider. It has to have a lot of insight in the organisation. The rational goal model also places the manager centrally. He develops the organisation and makes it grow. The leadership style is often task oriented. This kind of organisation closely resembles Ouchi's description of a market organisation. Ouchi emphasises that in such organisations it is important to maximise the output. The organisational climate will be characterised by a strong goal oriented information flow.

In this brief analysis we placed in each field of the competing values framework an ideal type of organisation. The reader probably noticed that the models and types have elements in common. This can be explained by the fact that the different points of view have some underlying values in common. Each ideal type has its benefits and disadvantages. The analysis of these is not within the scope of this article. We only wished to show how an organisation evolves when values are attached.

Undoubtedly we find characteristics of each type in one organisation. It is our opinion that one series of characteristics will dominate and that this will be reflected in the organsational climate. We are also convinced that a congruity of the organisational climate with the above mentioned variables will lead to higher organisational effectiveness.

Usefulness of the organisational climate instrument

The basis of measures of organisational climate is the ideal of collecting useful information through the whole course of an organisational development programme. The questionnaire can, together with other instruments, be used as a diagnostic and evaluative instrument through the whole of an organisational development process. Information about organisational climate draws attention to problems where corrective actions may be sought. It is therefore important to relate the scores on each scale, in concert with the client organisation, with concrete events. In this way we can gain an insight into the organisational climate of that organisation. These data can function as a starting point to give advice on possible changes which can be made in the organisation to achieve greater effectivness. The direction of the change depends on the kind of organisation. It differs from organisation to organisation. A concrete knowledge of the organisational climate can help the manager to formulate a direction for change.

However, we must be aware that this is a provisional model for organisational effectiveness. Further research is continuing concerning the relationship between on the one hand organisational climate and on the other hand organisational structure, context, personnel policies and management strategy.

Subscale	k	coefficient	coefficient
		group 1	group 2
1 Support	10	0.86	0.90
2 Innovation	11	0.81	0.84
3 Respect for rules	10	0.75	0.70
4 Goal oriented information flow	8	0.81	0.87

TABLE 1: Number of items (k) and reliability coefficients
(a) of the subscales of OKIPO on two different groups
of organisations. (1 = real organisational climate; 2
= wanted organisational climate).

References

Abrahamsson, B: Bureaucracy or participation. The logic of organisation. London, Sage Publications, 1977.

Bouwen R, De Cock, G, De Witte,K: Organisatieklimaat. Betekenis en bruiikbarrheid van een concept. Tijdschrift voor economie en management. 1978, 2,3 231-248.

De Cock, G, Bouwen, R, De Witte, K and De Visch, J,: Handleiding bij de organisatieklimaatindex voor profit organisaties (OKIPO) en zijn verkorte vorm (VOKIPO). Acco, Leuven, februari 1984, 1985, 2e druk.

Degry, K: Organisatieklimaat in ziekenhuizen. Reconstructie van de vragenlijst en praktishce richtlijnen voor het gebruik ervan. Niet- gepubliceerde licentiaatsverhandeling, Fac. der Psychologie en Pedagogische wetenschappen, K.UY. Leuven, 1982.

De Visch, J Organisatieklimaat: Een kritische studie van het concept en zijn relaties met organisatievariabelen, ontwikkeling van een theoretisch denkkader en toekomtsperspectieven. Niet gepubliceerde licentiaatsverhandeling, Fac. der Psychologie en Pedagogische Wetenscahppen, K.U. Leuven, 1983.

De Witte, K: Organisatieklimaat in Ziekenhuizen. Studie over het verband van organisatieklimaat met het funktioneren van de direkties en de overlegstrukturen. Niet gepubliceerde doctoraatsverhandeling onder leiding van Prof. G. De Cock., Fac. der Psychologie en Pedagogishce Wetenschappen, 1985.

Driesen, J: Constructie van een meetinstrument voor de perceptie van organisatieklimmat in ziekenhuizen. Niet gepubliceerde licentiaatsverhandeling, Fac. der Psychologie en Pedagogische wetenschappen, K U Leuven, 1979.

Handy, C B: Understanding organisations. Harmondsworth, Penguin Books Ltd. 1981.

Harrison, R: How to describe your organisation. Harvard Business Review Sept-Oct. 1972.

Katz, D and Kahn R L: The social psychology of organisation. New York, Wiley, 1978.

Lawrence, P R and Lorsch, J W: Organisation and environment. Harvard Business School, Division of research, Boston, 1967.

Mintzberg, Hz. Organisation design. Fashion or Fit? Harvard Business Review, 1981, 59, 103-116.

Ouchi, W G: Markets, bureaucracies and clans. Administrative Science Quarterly, 1980, 25, 855-866.

Payne, R L and Pheysey, D C Stern's organisational climate index: A reconceptualisation and application to business organisations. Organisational Behaviour and Human Performance, 1971, 6, 77-78.

Quinn, R E and Rohbaugh, J A: Spatial model of effectiveness criteria, towards a competing values approach to organisational analysis.

Steers, R N: Organisational effectiveness. A behavioural view. Santa Monica, Goodyear Publishing Company, 1977, 122p.

Stern, G G: People in context. Measuring person and environment congruence in education and industry. New York, J. Wiley and Sons, 1970.

Srivasta, S et al.: Job satisfaction and productivity. Cleveland, Department of Organisational Behaviour, 1975, XVI.

Chapter Four

INCULTURE : THE ORGANISATIONAL CHARACTER OF INC

B Hennestad

Introduction

The aim of this paper is to conceptualise and demonstrate how an organisation can be conceived as having a separate ideational system. This system is identified and described as an organisational character or paradigm consisting of a set of basic assumptions. It is demonstrated that the organisational character is not a static system, but rather a piece of "living history." The creating and recreating forces are identified as residing in contradictions constituted by the multicultural reality of the organisation, as well as the contradiction between culture and social structure.

The empirical basis for the analysis is mainly drawn from a case study reported elsewhere (Hennestad and Lovdal 1984). The name of the company - "INC" - is invented for the purpose of this paper, but the real name melts together with the Norwegian word for culture as INCulture.

Meeting an organisation - glimpses of a character.

We left the taxi outside a group of buildings on the outskirts of the city and had to choose between several entrances. In the hallway we spotted a modest sign picturing a snail and having the initials INC inscribed - the "snail" proved later to be a petrified octopus. Following the direction indicated by the sign, we traversed a corridor with a small post office and a small bank and finally entered the door of what we already knew to be a highly successful marketing oriented Research Institute in the oil exploring industry. However, as the octopus, INC had its tentacles inside a lot of other buildings which we later came to know as "the garage", the "church building", the "barracks" and others.

Having arrived, the scene changed dramatically, and we remembered how Maccoby (1976) compared the sensation of being inside a corporation for the first time with walking into a Mexican village for the first time. We were kindly and efficiently received, and the people we were set up to meet knew who we were and roughly why they should meet us. Everybody seemed to answer openly and bravely even to rather touchy questions. Meetings seemed to take place in an open and confronting style. Furthermore, when something of crucial importance to INC happened, as it did the very first days we were there, we were immediately invited to the ad hoc meetings of a highly confidential character that were set up. The meetings were thought to provide useful information for us, and people also as a matter of course helped us to rearrange our schedule by cancelling interviews and making new appointments. All major groups of the organisation were presented in these meetings, and during the assessment of the situation and possible alternatives for action, the managing director seemed more like an attentive listener, asking follow-up questions, rather than the person "running the show". The atmosphere was rather one of a collective, seeking solutions in spite of minor confrontations and disagreements.

The general impression gained from seeing how these meetings were arranged, and also from the formal and informal discussions with members of the organisation as well as our attendance and participation in other meetings, was one of vital energies unfolding and forceful action taking place. It certainly seemed a busy place - at all times of the day, and night; week days as well as weekends. Seriously as well as humorously it was also pointed out to us that being busy was important; details were not to be bothered with, a desktop should be messy.

The members of INC also expressed pride and self esteem on behalf of the company: they emphasised that INC and working at INC was something really special. They also expressed the view that it was an excellent company in its field; its research was outstanding and the delivered products were good if not better than those delivered by their competitors - an opinion, it proved later, that was not always fully shared by their customers. INC was held to be an excellent company by those we met and was also seen as performing a function that was an important one to the nation.

We were also told continuously that it was a sad thing that the company was so scattered; it has experienced rapid growth, and many of our contacts thought that there were too many people they did not know and too many unfamiliar faces. After telling us about the relatively substantial amount of organised sports activities and the numerous formal (and repetitive) and informal parties, people tended to reflect upon the importance of sticking together in view of the continuous risks of being split apart that INC faced. Some of the members also told us about the fun and hardship involved in the data collecting sea expeditions. The long term impact these expeditions had on interpersonal work relations were also emphasised. We were told that the building, big enough to house them all, represented the future ideal state that the INC'ers longed for. They also hoped for clarification from the government, on which role it wanted INC to play.

In short, we sensed a group of people who were characterised by confidence in themselves who displayed a lot of vital energies within some kind of common frame, and we knew that the company had proved successful in business terms. It seemed doubtful that a pure formal perspective on organisations (Blau and Scott 1962) would help to dig deeper into understanding the dynamics of such an organisation. On the contrary, Silverman's (1970) position that "action arises out of meaning", seemed to make sense: it seemed as if, as Clifford Geertz (1973) puts it, social actions are comments on more than themselves; that "meaning resides in the acts", or as argued by Philip Selznic (1957), that organisations can develop beyond their formal framework and become as he puts it; "infused with value". From this position it is tempting to make a footnote by citing Clifford Geertz (1973) once more: "It is not worth it as Thoreau said, to go around the world to count the cats of Zanizibar."

Krober and Parsons (1958) opposed the view that meaning was meshed into the social system, and proposed that there was a conceptually separate ideational system, or that an analytical distinction had to be made between social and cultural systems. This view is not reflected in an emerging amount of the literature on management and organisation. The importance of "deep structure" (Dandrige et.al 1980),or an underlying structure of meaning (Jelinek et.al. 1983) shaping experiences, channelling behaviour and thereby also affecting the performance of the organisation (Wilkins 1983) is being emphasised. We therefore aimed to dig a bit deeper INCulture.

Digging deeper

The answer to what is hiding in the overt behaviour displayed by the organisation members and its observers, should be sought in man's need for meaning. There is, as Geertz points out, "an information gap": "Between what our body tells us and what we need to know in order to function, there is a vacuum we must fill." "People need a continuous sense of what the reality is all about" (Pettigrew 1979), and the gap between the raw data of life and our minds has to be bridged by some kind of models for perceiving, organising and acting (Goodenough 1961). Some kind of models or forms are necessary for the intelligibility of life, or as Simmel (1967, p.204) has put it: "aspects of reality can be grasped as possible objects of experience only if they fall under some constitutive form". So, man is an animal suspended in the webs of significance he himself has spun, to borrow a phrase from Geertz.

However, meaning is tacit and taken-for-granted (Bate 1984), and it does not lend itself easily to discovery. Furthermore, the elusive character of the system of meaning is also due to the fact that it covers most aspects of life. The epistemological problems of conceptualising an organisational system of meaning fruitfully for exploration, are therefore considerable. Several researches have suggested that we should conceive organisational culture as a set of basic assumptions underlying the manifest aspects of the organisation. Wilkins (1983) proposes that assumptions about work means and work ends as well as reward assumptions are fruitful areas to focus on for the purpose of capturing important aspects of the culture of an organisation. Somewhat related to this is the approach adopted by W.Gibb Dyer (1982) and Edgar Schein (1983; 1984) building on Kulckhohn's conception of culture as presented in Kluchkhohn and Strodtbeck (1961). It is suggested that organisations meet the human need for meaning, order and consistency by developing paradigms that tie together basic assumptions. Categories that reflect important basic

assumptions are those about human nature, human
relationships, the nature of human activity, the
nature of reality, truth, and the relationship to the
environment. The idea is that the organisation
culture paradigms are adapted versions of broader
culture paradigms, and further that these assumptions
reflect human problems for which people at all times
and all places have had to find solutions. This has
been coined "the universal but variable" thesis (Bate
1984). Schein also presents the results from two
different case studies in which there are found to be
substantial differences in basic assumptions, and he
emphasises that the patterns of manifest behaviour
also were different in these two organisations.

These conceptions of organisational culture have
inspired and influenced our interpretation of INC as a
system of meaning. The interpreting process was built
upon data from observing staff meetings and planning
sessions, interaction with the members of the
organisation through casual conversations and loosely
structured interviews and through the study of
documents from the organisation, company (external and
internal) newsletters etc. The themes that were
explored emerged through cycles in which data
collection, data analysis and feedback were interwoven
(Glaser and Strauss 1968; Braten et al. 1983; Smircich
1983b). Non traditional techniques like the use of
animal metaphors (Berg 1983) and the writing of an
imaginary letter to a friend that should take over the
job of the informant were also employed to elicit
assumptions.

Glimpses of an organisational ethos

"Aggressive Self Esteem"

Through these cycles of data gathering and data
analysis emerged the woolly contours of an
organisational character or ethos. The picture was
not clear cut nor expressed in slogans as suggested in
the management literature (e.g. Deal and Kennedy 1983;
Peters and Waterman 1983). However it is doubtful
that the models and concepts people use are contained
in the mind as clear cut concepts ready for
presentation (Eden, Sims and Jones 1979). Neither is
the meaning embedded solely in words (Marshall and
MacLean 1985), as is the main medium of the
researcher, but is implicit in a range of symbolic
means, as well as in the wholeness of the situation;
meaning is "being in relation", as Linda Smircich puts

it (Smircich 1983c). The framework of the organisational paradigm (Brown 1978), its set of basic assumptions (Schein 1984) or its "frame of meaning" (Giddens 1976) is based on "interpretations" of interpretations, it is grounded in the everyday world of the organisation members and validated or rendered credible through feedback cycles.

We did not find slogans that embedded the core of the organisational character. Neither did we find any evidence of well-known stories in which core values were implicit, the existence of which is claimed by some researchers in the field (Clark 1972, Martin 1983, Martin et al. 1983). The culture was rather found to be elusive and implicit in the mundane, enacted and spontaneous realities of the organisation. This does not however exclude the existence of ritualistic functions being performed by such phenomenon as meetings (Smircich 1983), feasts and celebrations (Deal and Kennedy 1983), which were aspects we also found to play a role in forming and sustaining the culture at INC. The pattern of basic assumptions which dimly emerged from our interactions can loosely be described as follows:

1. The shaping of experiences and channelling of behaviour at INC seemed to rest upon an assumption of INC and INC'ers as performing important tasks. The knowledge produced and the services delivered by INC are considered to be of utmost importance to the oil exploiting industry and consequently to the welfare of the nation. INC are however operating in an environment that is - according to prevailing assumptions - characterised by latent and occasionally manifest hostility. Some especially influential actors in the government research systems do not share INC perceptions of their own role, and at times are even considered to envy their success. INC'ers pretend they do not like, or at least are tired of "wars" but simultaneously they hold it to be important to master their own destiny, and that it is possible to fight back.

2. When it is possible to be master of their own destiny, this is mainly because INC and INC'ers are outstanding in what they are doing. With excellent researchers as their crucial resource they are delivering high quality products that are better than those of their competitors.

INC'ers consider work to be fun, that being busy is fine, and that there are no sharp divisions between work time and spare time. It is the executive part of work that is appreciated; doing rather than planning. However, the performance and the results should correspond to high professional standards of quality.

3.   Results are achieved to a large extent because people are willing and able to take on responsibility. This ability, and willingness, is however felt to presuppose and to justify freedom - at least from the feeling of being checked and controlled. Furthermore, and partly related to the assumptions about freedom and control, INC'ers do not take on responsibility for the situation of others, unless they take the initiative - and in that case "doors will be opened." So, newcomers have to learn the hard way. It is therefore seen to be important to give feedback, or confront, when something is felt to be wrong. This should however be done without screaming too loud, or being nasty, even if that is accepted from some people.

In a study of the GEM corporation, Dyer (1982) notes that it operates on the interlocking assumptions that: 1) ideas come ultimately from individuals; 2) people are responsible, motivated, and capable of governing themselves; however, truth can only be pragmatically determined by "fighting" things out and testing in groups; 3) such fighting is possible because the members of their organisation view themselves as a family who take care of each other. Ultimately, this makes it safe to fight and be competitive. Schein (1984) has observed another organisation with a different paradigm: 1) truth comes ultimately from older, wiser, better educated, higher status members; 2) people are capable of loyalty and discipline in carrying out directives; 3) relationships are basically linear and vertical; 4) each person has a niche that is his or her territory that cannot be invaded; and 5) the organisation is a "solidary unit" that will take care of its members.

It is clear that INC is different from both these organisation cultures, although closer to GEM Corporation than the other. However, the point is not to make a comparison, but to demonstrate that organisations also consist of paradigms or systems of meaning. As Schein points out, there are different sets of manifest behaviour. The manifest behaviour of the GEM Corporation is for example characterised by a general air of informality, whilst the organisation observed by Schein is permeated by a general air of formality. Nonetheless, behavioural differences make no sense, until the underlying system of meaning has been interpreted. Cultural artifacts are the manifestations of culture and must not be confused with cultural content.

INCulture; the living history

The culture of INC seems to be strong in the sense that relatively many important and nonconflicting assumptions are widely shared among the members of the organisation (Sathe 1983). However, there is a need to regard this conception of unity and a strong culture as problematic by analysing the data from different perspectives. First of all, it is important to realise that the character of INC is not a given, static system. It is rather a piece of "living history", to borrow a phrase from Malinowski. The character of INC has been socially constructed by past actions and interactions of its present and previous members (Berger and Luckman 1967). It has been created during a process of structuration (Giddens 1979), in which the existing structure of meaning constrains the ongoing production of that of tomorrow.

Consequently, the symbolic forms of today include the sediments of past interactions. The culture of an organisation is held to provide continuity, control, integration and identity to its members (Louis 1983) and to offer solutions to problems of external adaptation (Schein 1984). In the character of INC the struggles or early days seem to appear dimly. In these days the company leads an insecure existence, new threats are popping up continuously and the company has to change locations periodically. There also seem to be traces of the many other struggles against integration with other institutes during recent stages of its history. One of the previous managing directors put it this way: "INC has acquired the shape of a raindrop always having had to move against the stream". During the insecure existence of the first five to six years of its life, INC moved to another town, but also in the following ten year period its offices have become scattered and the frequent change of some of its locations, has resulted in a desire for "reunion in one house". The amount of parties and celebration, the high degree of participation in organised INC sporting activities alongside the espoused obsession of "keeping together" is seen as a reflection of these partly externally imposed threats.

The culture of an organisation is by many authors seen to be an obstacle to change due to its resilience (Marshall and MacLean 1985; Deal and Kennedy 1982; Schwartz and Davis 1981). This might be what planned change is concerned with since cultural processes are taking place "behind the back" of the members of an organisation due to the taken for grantedness of meaning. (Argyris 1978). Change is however going on all the time. We have tried to demonstrate that today's organisational character is a product of the past; a piece of living history. This product constitutes a precarious frame constraining the unfolding social processes creating tomorrow's organisational character, rendering INC a piece of living and emerging history. To explore the dialectics of the latent future it is necessary to move beyond the notion of a unitary organisational culture. The assumptions described are held to encapsulate both the existing character of INC, and the grains of contradictions.

The creating and recreating of INC's character

INC exists as some kind of totality. As a company it is an institution by law, it possesses structural arrangements which are enforced to varying degrees, and these as well as management activities serve as points of reference (Smircich and Morgan 1982) for the development of native understanding. These features are therefore seen to loosely encapsulate INC as a totality, still allowing for a variety of organisational characters to develop. The totality can be perceived and enacted (Weick 1979) in different ways having different but real results, as illustrated by Thomas's:.."if people define situations as real, they become real in their consequences". By suggesting an INC organisational character we have however proposed that there are common ways of perceiving and organising experiences and contradictions that represent grains in the restlessness of the character, which are to some extent "in the background" of that unity. Revealing these contradictions is believed to shed light on the several possible paths which may develop in the future. These contradictions are found in the multicultural reality of the organisation as well as in the multicultural reality of its members. They are also found to be related to the different nature of relationships that exist between different groups of members of the organisation and the system of meaning reflected in the organisational character.

The multicultural reality of INC

INC seems to mean a lot to its members as a source of identity and a point of reference for the development of basic assumptions operating in the organisational setting. These members are, however, at any time products of and members of various cultural settings as emphasised amongst others by Sorrokin, who states..." It represents the coexistence of cultural systems - partly harmonious, partly indifferent, partly contradictory to one another - plus the coexistence of many congeries that have somehow entered the individual's local culture and settled there" (Sorrokin 1966: 32,33). The background of INC'ers differ socially, educationally, geographically. They are parts of different settings; unions, families and neighbourhoods again encompassing other members inhabiting multicultural realities. We do not have the space nor the data to explore the wholeness of INC members' cultural realities in depth. Departmental variations in underlying assumptions were however identified. These probably derive from such factors as differences in task, office location and also express themselves in different styles and rituals. We will, however, concentrate on some educational and professional background factors that create traceable subcultural tendencies that could have important implications.

Broadly speaking there are two kinds of researchers at INC: the chartered engineer and the one having a research degree from a university. Subcultural differences are known to exist amongst researchers/product developers in "high tech" companies (Gregory 1983). At INC both types are found in all departments fulfilling generally speaking the same kind of functions and occupying the same kind of positions, but INC'ers are very aware of there being a difference between the two groups. Indeed, they make mostly friendly jokes about it. A common attitude seems to be that the chartered engineer is more readily able to adjust his or her ambitions and professional standards according to the economy of a particular project, whilst the university type of researcher is geared towards academic standards and finds it harder not to comply with these. The chartered engineers are also more at ease with group work projects, whilst the other group tend to prefer to work alone; being humorously pictured by the others as the old fashioned geologist carrying a rucksack and with hammer and chisel in his hands. The marketing orientation, sustained by the present top management and some of the most influential old stagers, is also met by greater scepticism amongst this group, who argue that it will easily result in a repetitive work situation and a less interesting professional knowledgebase. This argument is being challenged by the view that a marketing orientation will create an economic platform for the interesting and academically rewarding kind of projects. Those supporting this stand are - apart from the managing director - those acknowledged by others as the entrepreneurs who often have a background as chartered engineers. This acknowledgement could partly account for the way that the contradiction between these different orientations seems to represent latent rather than manifest tensions, as there seems to be little heavy disagreement resulting in bitterness related to the actual decisions in this area.

The "veterans" or "old stagers", a group of researchers who have stayed long with the company and occupy a special status, constitute another subcultural phenomenon. They are mentioned - by name as good informants and as typical INC'ers by the other organisational members. To some extent they are held to be different, as the newer members tend to state that..."things do not matter so much to me as to them". With some frustration they are also said to operate as if the company still only has 50 employees (it now has more than three times that number). The old stagers are formally as well as through informal networks heavily involved in the management of the company. They possess important positions for instance as heads of departments, or perhaps even more importantly, they replace the heads of department when they are away, which is very often. The "old stagers" tend to have a chartered engineer background, their INC identity is very strong, and they are concerned with freedom of action for INC, and are often in favour of growth. The adherence to the INC character is strongest in this group, which would correspond closely to what Martin and Siehl (1983) have labelled an enhancing subculture, with the exception that they assume it to be an organisational enclave, whilst at INC, the members are scattered in several departments.

The organisational character and the organisational members; beyond unity.

The existence of a multicultural reality and its inherent contradictions and dialectics partly account for the fact that members of a particular social system do not become cultural replicants. The nature of this relationship between the cultural system and the individual is of particular interest for the exploration of the dialectics and dynamics of that system. The location of culture has been a matter of basic dispute in the social sciences which is closely related to this issue. Goodenough, a leading anthropologist in ethnoscience of the "cognitive school" holds culture to consist of whatever one has to know or believe in order to operate in a manner acceptable to the society's members, and defines it as "a system of standards for perceiving, evaluating and acting" (Goodenough 1971 p41). Clifford Geertz, a leading anthropologist in the "symbolic" school, strongly opposes the idea that "cultural is located in the minds or hearts of men", a view he holds to be "the main source of muddlement in contemporary anthropology" (1973:11). "Culture is public, because meaning is. It does not exist in someone's head", are arguments he puts forward emphasising that culture is public, not private (Geertz 1973:10,12) Other authors in the field point out that Goodenough has a conception of culture as a composite of what is shared and public (Keesing 1973:85) and will not acknowledge that the difference between the two is significant, as claimed by Geertz (Sanday 1979). Their view is a less antagonistic one; "Culture must be thinkable and learnable as well as liveable" (Keesing 1987:86).

In suggesting a framework for the study of organisational culture, Allaire and Firsirotu (1984) choose a way around this epistemological problem. They rely upon a symbolic perspective, but compromise by proposing and emphasising the (Goodenough) term "cultural competence" to connote the various modes of personal integrations of the public system of symbols.

At INC the "old stagers" could - by exaggeration - be characterised as cultural replicas, somewhat like Whyte's "Organisation man", or Maccoby's "Company man". Those members of the organisation that perform "supportive" or "helpfunctions"; secretaries, technicians, laboratory assistants and the like, seem to relate to the organisational character in a different fashion. To a large extent the INC'ers occupying these kind of positions espouse the same assumptions and share the same overt behavioural style as the above mentioned; they do, however, tend to talk about INC and related issues in more rarified and distant terms. It is also particularly amongst these people that one finds the emphasis that a typical INC'er is a researcher. Furthermore, it is organisational members from their category, especially their most vocal spokesman, that point out that the work environment at INC can be rather "tough" and one of them stated that working at INC was "no f.... Sunday school". This could mean that it is not only a question of which degree of integration that exists between the individual and the culture, but that lack of integration could indicate some form of cultural alienation. At least, we suggest that there is a need for such a conception characterising the possible forms of relationships between the organisational member and the organisational culture.

Even if there are indications that these people have a more estranged relationship to the organisational character, it could be hypothesised that it would influence their personal culture, their espoused theories and overt behaviour. As there does not exist any vivid cultural alternative, the subcultures being more or less variations of a theme - the personal organisational culture is acquired by traversing artifacts of the strong INC culture. Furthermore, important features of the culture are being imposed by dominant members of the organisation, who operate a kind of "model" monopoly (Braten 1973). However, we should not immediately infer that the individuals relationship to the cultural system is straightforward. One example that might serve to illustrate this, is a technician that was a union spokesman and who had served a relatively short time with INC. He was amongst those being most critical of the values of the traditional INC culture, emphasising that it was a "researcher oriented culture", and that it has a dark side with many negative factors. Shortly afterwards - on a very nice spring Friday - we found that on his own initiative he worked overtime until nine o'clock in the evening before visiting a friend in another town by plane. He had to finish some important work!

There is also a problematic relationship between the cultural manifestations and the cultural content, that demonstrates the difficulties in revealing the kind of relationship between an individual or a group and the system of meaning. The researchers at INC had adopted a seemingly easy going "style", a bit messy and "woolly", but with extremely hard work periods at times of a project deadline. Now, it could be proposed that this rhythm, or lack of rhythm, follows from, and also suits, the nature of their work – creative periods at times, but more straightforward and routinised at other times. However, some but far from all, participants in other occupational groups adopted the same behavioural style. It is doubted whether this had the same meaning to them as to the researchers. It could be proposed that they adopted this behaviour because it attracted them or doing so made the work here different from that in other organisations. However, even if this style might suit the work of a researcher, it did not suit the work of the administrator, and to some extent this also seemed to be a source of strain.

It seems especially to be the old stagers, this is a relative concept, who have a nonalienated and integrated relationship to the cultural system as described. It is their own history that is reflected in that culture, and it seems to be some sort of congruency between their personal culture and the cultural system of the organisation, between the models they use and those embedded in the artifacts of INC. In the long run that might not be the supportive source it is often held to be. It is the model of the prevailing culture that is the source for the search for solutions to problems. However, the culture reflects past solutions to past problems. This could mean that it is difficult to think outside the cultural framework of meaning, and that even thinking about change is shaped by the culture (Marshall and McLean 1985).

It could endanger the inability to perform what Watzlawick (Watzlawick et al. 1974) coin second order change, leaving first order change as the only kind of change the organisation is capable of performing. First order change involves change within a category; adjustments within a set of ground rules, whilst second order change occurs if basic assumptions change. From an organisational point of view that could be tragic in the long run, if the environment changes considerably, the culture would in that case constitute a blockage to the planned and conscious implementation of new standards and models.

There are indications that this might be the case.
The old stagers did not seem to realise the need for a
formal administrative structure in the shape of better
management information (and control) systems. This
was a need urged by the management as a consequence of
heavy growth and in some cases of over expenditure.
The growth in size was rationally realised, and
therefore, an understanding of a need for such systems
was espoused. They were met by a ritualistic reaction
and ways were found around them. The younger
generation on the other hand seemed to be more
understanding of the needs behind more structure.
Some of them also expressed the view that the old
stagers thought and operated as if INC still had 50
employees, but the actual number had increased to
three times that much. Furthermore there was the view
that the environment is hostile, and that INC is
performing well, and better than its competitors.
There were indications that changes have occurred in
this field without the basic assumption having
adjusted accordingly. That also seems to constitute
the future development.

The cultural and the structural system - contradiction or congruity?

The traditional emphasis has been on freedom and
responsibility. As stated above, the management had
realised a need for tighter administrative systems for
information and follow up. These systems were
especially supported and enforced by an "outsider"
hired as Director of Administrative functions. There
was an espoused support for the aims of tighter
controls, but in actual practice organisation members
do not seem to consider control legitimate. The
filling-in of forms, and accounting for minor expenses
and explaining the need for this and that, were rather
felt as an insult. Organisation members felt that
they were productive, clever, profitable and
hardworking, and therefore felt entitled to be seen as
responsible persons, capable of making judgements.
This situation was creating manifest as well as latent
tensions in the organisation.

This observation proves the value of identifying the
cultural system as conceptually separate from the
structural system, because their relationship can be
characterised by the cultural system legitimising the
(socio) structure system which supports the cultural
system. On the other hand, the relationship between
these systems could also be a conflicting one

characterised by tension (Allaire and Firsirotu 1984).
As pointed out by Geertz (1973:144) these systems are
capable of a wide range of modes of integration of
which the simple isomorphic mode is but a limiting
case. Conceiving organisations containing symbolic
and instrumental components, Pfeffer (1981:6)
emphasises that these "have different variables,
different processes and are themselves imperfectly
linked". Geertz also holds the incongruities between
these systems to be a major source of social change
(Geertz 1973:144/169). Our study of INC was not a
longitudinal one. However, grains of change seem to
reside in the tension between these systems as
described above. At the time of the study the
administrative procedures to some extent seemed to
develop towards being rituals embedding rather
negative assumptions about the members' relationships
to the company. However, the resilience and power of
culture seemed to lead to the culture manifesting
itself in the project organisation rather than in the
basic organisation. This was made possible in part
because the projects had their own budgeting system.

Concluding comments

We described the organisational culture of INC by
identifying a set of shared basic assumptions. The
paradigm constituted by these assumptions was labelled
"aggressive self esteem" trying to encapsulate the
character or ethos of the organisational culture.
This character has been socially constructed by the
present and past members of INC. That is one of the
reasons why we - borrowing a phrase from Malinowski -
label it "a piece of living history". Another reason
is that grains of the processes constituting the
future culture can be traced in today's culture, but
to do that one has to seek beyond the unitary image
presented by the description of the organisational
character. By pointing at contradictions within the
totality of INC, we are drawing on a dialectical view
(e.g. Benson 1977). Such contradictions are found to
be constituted by such phenomena as the multicultural
realities of the members of the organisation, the
subcultural tendencies and the different modes of
integration between the personal and the
organisational culture as well as the tensions created
by the relationship between the cultural and the
structural system. There seems to be a paradox in
posing a set of shared basic assumptions and
simultaneously identifying these contradictions.
However, a person's character can be identified as

something specific and different from others, but at the same time it is able to reflect different perspectives and to even encapsulate contradictory beliefs. That is also the case with a social system; the assumptions that are shared exist in some kind of foreground, but these must also be seen against a background of contradictions. These contradictions constitute the dynamic vitality of the organisation representing latent evolution, adaptation and change. So does, of course, the interpersonal dialogue (Braten 1983) and individual reflexivity (Winch 1958). It is through these processes that new perspectives emerge and new paths are discovered and from these the organisation might develop some kind of requisite variety (Ashby 1956) to meet changing demands. As it is, however, these change processes take place behind the backs of the members of the organisation meaning that they have no control and little conscious influence on the direction the changes take.

References

Allaire, Y and Firsirotu, M E: Theories of
Organisation Culture. Organisation Studies 5 (3),
1984

Argyris, C and Schön D: Organisational Learning: A
Theory of Action Perspective. Reading, Mass:
Addison-Wesley 1978.

Bate, P: The Impact of Organisation Culture on
Approaches to Organisation Problem Solving.
Organisation Studies 5 (1), 1984: 43-66.

Benson, K: Organisations: A Dialectical View.
Administrative Science Quarterly 22, 1977.

Berg, P O: Corporate Culture Development: Paper
presented at meeting between Nordic Schools of
Business Administration, Copenhagen, August 24-27,
1983.

Berger, P L and Luckman, T: The Social Construction of
Reality. Harmondsworth: Penguin Books 1967.

Blau, P M and Scott, R W: The Concept of Formal
Organisation. Novato, Calif: Chandler and Sharp
1982.

Brown, R H: Bureaucracy as Praxis: Towards a Political
Phenomenology of Formal Organisations.
Administrative Science Quarterly 23, 1978.

Braten, S: Model Monopoly and Communication. Acta
Sociologica 16 (2), 1973: 98-107.

Braten, S: Dialogens vilkar i samfunnet. Oslo:
Universiteforlaget 1983.

Braten, S, Hennestad, B W and Wenstop, F: Kognitiv
Kartlegging av organisation oq datakultur.
Arbeidsnotat 83/7 Oslo: Bedriftsokonomisk
Institute 1983.

Clark, B R: The Organisational Saga in Higher
Education. Administrative Science Quarterly 17,
1972:178-184.

Dandridge, T C, Mitroff J and Joyce W F:
Organisational Symbolism: A Topic to Expand

Organisational Analysis. Academy of Management
Journal 5 (1), 1980

Deal, T E and Kennedy, A A: Corporate Cultures.
Reading, Mass: Addison-Wesley 1982.

Dyer, W G: Culture in Organisations. WP 129-82.
Boston, Mass: Massachusetts Institute of
Technology 1982.

Eden, D, Jones S and Sims D: Thinking in
Organisations. London: MacMillan Press 1979.

Geertz, C: The Interpretation of Cultures. New York,
N.Y.: Basic Books 1973.

Giddens, A: New Rules of Sociological Method. London:
Hutchinson 1976.

Glaser, B G and Strauss, A L: The Discovery of
Grounded Theory. Hawthorne, N.Y. Aldine
Publishing Co. 1967

Goodenough, W H: Comments on Cultural Evolution.
Daedalus 90, 1961:521-528.

Gregory, K L: Native View Paradigms: Multiple Culture
Conflicts in Organisations. Administrative
Science Quarterly 28, 1983

Jelinek, M , Smircich, L and Hirsch P: Introduction:
A Code of Many Colours. Administrative Science
Quarterly 28, 1983

Keesing, R M: Theories of Culture. Annual Review of
Anthropology 1974: 73-97

Kluckholm, F R and Strodtecck,F L, Evanston III:
Variations in Value Orientations. Row Peterson
1961

Kroeber, A L and Parsons, T: The Concept of Culture
and of Social System": American Sociological
Review 23, 1958

Louis, M R: Organisations as Culture Gearing Milieux.
Pondy et al (eds.): Organisation Symbolism,
Greenwick, Conn: JAI Press 1983.

Maccoby, M: The Gamesman. New York, N.Y. Bantam Books
1976.

Marshall, J and McLean, A: Exploring Organisational
    Culture as a Route to Organisational Change.
    Hammond (ed): Current Research in Management.
    London: Francis Pinter 1985.

Martin, J: Stories and Scripts in Organisational
    Settings. Astor & Isenled (eds): Cognitive
    Social Psychology. New York N.Y.: 1982:225-230.

Martin, J and Siehl, C: Organisation Culture and
    Counterculture: An Uneasy Symbiosis.
    Organisational Dynamics 12 (2), August 1983.

Martin, J et al: The Uniqueness Paradox in
    Organisational Stories. Administrative Science
    Quarterly 28, 1983

Oakes, G: G Simmel Translated and Edited. Manchester
    University Press 1980.

Peters, T J and Waterman R H: In Search of Excellence.
    New York, N.Y. Harper & Row 1982

Pettigrew, A M: On Studying Organisation Culture.
    Administrative Science Quarterly, December 1979.

Pfeffer, J: Management as Social Action: The Creation
    and Maintenance of Organisational Paradigms.
    Research in Organisational Behaviour 3, JAI Press
    1981.

Sanday, P R: The Ethnographic Paradigm(s).
    Administrative Science Quarterly, December 1979.

Sathe, V: Implications of Corporate Culture: A
    Manager's Guide to Action. Organisational
    Dynamics 12 (2), 1983.

Schein, E: Coming to a New Awareness of Organisational
    Culture. Sloan Management Review, Winter 1984.

Schwartz, H and Davis, S M: Matching Corporate Culture
    and Business Strategy. Organisation Dynamics,
    Summer 1981

Selznick, P: Leadership in Administration. New York,
    N.Y. Harper & Row 1957

Silverman, D: The Theory of Organisations. London:
    Heinemann 1981.

Smircich, L: The Concept of Culture in Organisational
   Analysis. Administrative Science Quarterly 28
   September 1983

Smircich, L, and Morgan, G (ed):   Studying
   Organisations as Cultures. Beyond Method.   London
   Stage 1983

Smircich, L: Leadership: The Management of Meaning.
   Journal of Applied Behavioural Science 18 (3)
   1982:257-273

Sorrokin, P A: Sociological Theories of Today. New
   York, N.Y.: Harper & Row International 1966.

Watzlawick, P: Weackland, J A and Fisch R Change:
   Principles of Problem Formulation and Problem
   Resolution. New York N.Y. Norton 1974.

Weick, K: The Social Psychology of Organising
   Reading, Mass: Addison-Wesley 1979.

Wilkins, A L: The Cultural Audit: A Tool for
   Understanding Organisations.   Organisational
   Dynamics, Autumn 1983.

Winch, P: The Idea of Social Science.   London:
   Routledge & Kegan Paul 1958.

Chapter Five

ORGANISATIONAL SURVEYS AND PARTICIPATIVE MANAGEMENT
APPROACHES

K F Ackermann

Introduction

Organisational surveys are a neglected management tool
in Germany. A very small number of companies use them
in a systematic way for human resource management
decisions. The following contribution discusses
organisational surveys in the framework of
participative management. It is argued that properly
designed and implemented organisational surveys will
improve management efficiency and effectiveness. The
core problem is how to use survey results once they
are in. Based on empirical research in German
companies, some approaches for turning results into
action are presented.

The Rise of Participative Management Approaches in Germany and Western Europe

"The German system produces tough, authoritarian
executives who do very little delegating." This
comment by an American on German managers in the
sixties seemed to be valid more or less for managers
in other European countries, too. In the same decade
Servant-Schreiber published his bestseller: "Le Defi
Americain" which stated an existing and still growing
management gap between Europe and USA. In order to
close this gap, more participation in decision-making
and leadership was proposed to the European managers.

Nowadays, participative management is in principal no
longer questioned. There are good reasons for its
application, in particular:

> political: realising industrial democracy
> economic: improving efficiency and goal
> accomplishment of the firm

psychological: strengthening work motivation and work satisfaction of the employees.

Considering, how and to what extent participative management could or should be realised in business, organisational surveys attract our attention as a powerful participative management tool.

Types of Participative Management Approaches

Participation, as this term is used in the present paper, is defined as "giving employees whose work and working situation are affected by organisational decisions taken by others, a say (a part) in one or more phases of the cycle of taking decisions. Thus, participation may bear upon e.g. defining a problem, assessing alternative solutions, taking a decision, designing strategic policies, evaluating actions taken, and so forth." (Thierry 1985).

There are various participative management approaches which differ, among others, in the type of participation they provide. When examining participation it is possible to distinguish between two main systems:

(1) Indirect systems of participation. These are characterised by the fact that members of the Workers Council are elected and should represent the interests of their constituency;

(2) Direct systems of participation. These systems allow employees to engage in participative activities on their own behalf.

Organisational surveys can serve as a direct participation tool, but can also support indirect systems of participation.

In Germany, indirect systems of participation prevail, while direct participation is less developed. Indirect participation has been criticised for not being able to motivate employees and satisfy higher level needs, for example: esteem, autonomy and self-actualisation need (Schanz 1983). Empirical research findings support the thesis that direct participation is superior in terms of more motivation and higher satisfaction (Thierry 1985). The conclusion is that indirect systems of participation should be supplemented by more direct participation.

Organisational surveys are expected to offer a feasible way for business.

The participative potential of organisational Surveys

Organisational surveys have a considerable potential for increased participation of the workers in decision-making. This becomes clear if the following criteria or dimensions of participation are considered from a management point of view:

(1) degree or stage of participation
    (from commmunication and consulting to co- and self- determination)
(2) domain of participation
    (information on facts versus value judgements on what is good or desirable)
(3) types of participation
    (indirect versus direct systems)
(4) decision phase of participation
    (participation in regard of one or more phases of decision-making, e.g. the search for alternatives, the evaluation of alternatives and, finally, the control of results).

Organisational surveys cover all these criteria and can provide maximum participation in all of them.

A management model for conducting organisational surveys

A simplified model for conducting organisational surveys which leads to action programmes is shown in Figure 1.

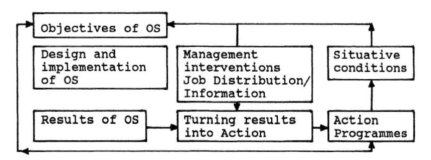

Figure 1: A Management Model for OS

1   The objectives of the organisation survey (OS) determine its design and implementation.

2   After implementation and application, survey results are produced.

3   Survey results are the inputs which are turned into action by means of a multi-step process. This process is or can be the subject of management interventions.

4   The output of the process under consideration consists of action programmes which will influence both the situative conditions under which OS takes place and the desired objectives.

Situative conditions will not only influence the objectives but also the manner of management interventions directed to the process of turning results into action.

Organisational reactions to survey results

Organisational Surveys are, in general, considered as a management tool. A rapidly growing number of publications deals with the question of how to get the data, while the use of survey results seems to attract less attention. The problem to be discussed in the present paper was formulated by David Sirota some years, ago: "Opinion Surveys: the results are in, what do we do with them?" Starke and Ferratt have shown that four types of organisational reactions are possible when the survey results are in:

.   Denying Results

.   Justifying Results

.   Allocating Results

.   Coping through Constructive Improvement

(1) Denying Results

The facts are disputed, the actuality or reality is denied or interpreted in a more favourable light. Organisations resort to this defence mechanism because it protects them, at least momentarily, from loss of esteem, confidence, and face. Moreover, denial appears to be a reasonable, first-shot strategy to save time and energy in actually connecting or improving the internal environment of the firm.

(2) Justifying Results

This reaction is characterised by the attempt to justify or rationalise the survey results. Typically, the organisation will try to diminish the significance of the data, for example, by pointing out that things could be even worse and that there are even poorer performers.

(3) Allocating Results

Organisations can allocate responsibility for the state of the internal environment to someone else or to an external agent, for example, to the company headquarters, to trade unions - that is an external attribution. This type of reaction often involves aggressive fault-finding and emotional assertions of blame.

(4) Coping through constructive improvement

Coping with survey results involves the following steps:

Should we do something?

Can we do something?

What alternatives are available?

What consequences are attached to each of the perceived courses of action in terms of inputs and outputs?

Designing and executing the action programme.

Nothing is said by Starke and Ferratt about how the process of turning survey results into action is or should be managed. The present paper analyses the state of the art of German firms as a first step for future improvements.

Empirical Research Findings

A survey on the state of the art of organisational surveys was conducted in 10 different German firms which had some experiences in the application of this management tool.

1. Goals and purposes of organisational surveys

In the literature, different goals and purposes of organisational surveys are mentioned. According to Figure 2, the diagnosis of organisational climate and the "identification of weakness and improvement of efficiency" are the most important, followed by the desire to improve information and communication within the organisation.

All the goals and purposes listed below are more or less closely related to that type of organisational reaction which was earlier described as "coping through constructive improvement".

The question is which influencing factors determine the desired goals and purposes of an organisational survey and how strong is their influence? Figure 3 shows that goal setting for organisational surveys is manager-oriented. In most cases, the attitudes to surveys, management guidelines and the preferred supervisory style are the main determinants. These determinants are also expected to dominate the basic decision on whether or not a survey should be conducted.

Goals/Purposes	IMPORTANCE			
	very	important	less	not
Diagnosis of organisational climate	6	3		
Identification of weakness and improvement of efficiency	5	3	1	
Improved information and communication	3	4	2	
Evaluation of changes in working conditions	2	1	3	3
Better cooperation between management and the workers' council	1	2	4	2
Controlling the perception and evaluation of the incentive system		6	2	1

Figure 2: Importance-rating of survey goals and purposes in 10 German companies (non response from 1)

Goal setting for surveys is influenced by	INFLUENCES				
	very strong	rather strong	rather weak	very weak	none
Attitude of superiors	5	3			
Management guidelines, supervisory style	4	4			
Economic situation of the company	3	4	1		
Organisational climate	3	4			1
Attitude of the workers council	2	4	2		
Size of company	1	2	3	1	1
Structure of company (organi sation structure, technology, production programme)		3	3	2	

Figure 3: The main determinants of survey goals and purposes in 10 German companies (non response from 2)

2. Turning survey results into action

Turning survey results into action requires a sequence of different steps or activities. Among them, problem analysis (why are the results as bad as they are?) and the design of action programmes for improvement are judged most frequently as "difficult" or even as "very difficult." The perceived difficulty of the other activities varies from company to company.

Activities of turning survey-results into action	Difficulty-rating			
	very difficult	rather difficult	rather easy	easy
Interpretation of survey-results and identification of problem areas		3	4	3
Problem analysis Search for explanation	1	7	2	
Search for more information	2	2	5	1
Planning of actions for problem solving	3	4	3	
Other activities				
Motivation to cooperate	1	3	5	1
Coordination	1	3	4	2

Figure 4: Difficulty-rating of main activities to turn survey results into action
(N = 10 German companies)

Our basic thesis is that the process of turning survey results into action is and should be effectively organised and managed. This can be done in different ways. Two types of management interventions are distinguished: First of all, management has to decide who should perform the activities necessary for turning survey results into action, and also, who should participate. We call this type of intervention "job distribution". The second type of management intervention relates to the information policy of the company. Decisions are necessary as to the receivers of information, the information channels, the content of information and so forth. All these management decisions are expected to have an important impact on the efficiency of the process.

a) Job distribution models

1. Internal versus external approaches

The process of turning survey results into action can be performed either internally by organisational members, or externally by consultants.

The external model is characterised as a "doctor-patient-model". The consultant as the doctor performs the diagnosis and, then, prescribes the medicine, which the patient, the company, has to swallow. The opposite case is characterised as a "self-cure-model". The company as the patient performs both the diagnosis and the therapy. Between these extremes, various mixed models are possible.

The empirical findings show that there is no clear preference in favour of the internal or the external model or for mixed internal-external approaches. All these models are in use:

            Doctor-patient-models : 3
            Self-cure-models   : 2
            Mixed models   : 4

Each of these models has specific advantages and disadvantages.

2. Centralisation versus decentralisation

The process of turning survey results into action can be performed either in a centralised way by the personnel department or in a decentralised way by the heads of the departments and individual line managers.

Instead of strict centralisation or strict decentralisation, team models prevail which provide cooperaton of personnel department experts and managers of the organisation units involved. The workers' council is often invited to participate. If survey results are highly detailed and relate to small units, the heads of these units are mainly responsible for problem analysis and for the design of action programmes. In general, they will decide whether the members of their unit are also allowed to participate.

3. Top-down versus bottom-up approaches

In the companies observed, the bottom-up approach seems to prevail.

b) Information models

Information is another important tool of management to influence the process of turning OS results into action. A rather selective information policy can be observed:

In all the companies under study, the detailed OS results were transmitted to the heads of the organisational units involved, but not always to their immediate superiors or to the personnel department.

In all these companies, the heads of the organisational units involved received the detailed OS results of their unit and the aggregated OS results for the whole company or larger units. In a very few cases, they also received OS results for organisational units at the same hierarchy level.

Different communication channels were used for informing superiors and subordinates.

c) The influence of situative variables

How the difficult process of turning survey results into action was managed in the companies observed, depended on situative variables such as the attitudes of superiors and of the workers' council. Other situative variables were of minor importance. The research findings are shown in more detail in Figure 5.

Process of turning survey-results into action is influenced by ...	Strength of influence				
	very strong	rather strong	rather weak	very weak	no influence
Attitude of superiors	6	2			
Attitude of workers' council	6	2			
Management guidelines and supervisory style	3	4			1
Organisational climate	2	5			1
Size of company	2	3	2		1
Attitude of work force	1	4	2		1
Economic situation of the company	1	2	3	1	1
*Structure of the company	1	2	2	1	2

*(organisation structure, technology, production programme)

Figure 5: Main determinants of managing the process of turning survey results into action (Sample: 10 German companies)

3. Evaluation of organisational surveys

(a) Experts, evaluation of survey-induced changes

Organisational surveys are evaluated in terms of actions and changes which are produced by them. In the present sample, major changes were observed, most frequently in decision-areas such as information and communication and, also, in performance appraisal and promotion procedures. (Figure 6).

Effects of survey induced actions in the area of ...	Extent of changes		
	high	low	no change
Information, communication	5	1	0
Performance evaluation, promotion systems.	4	2	0
Professional training of employees	3	3	0
Management training (Leadership behaviour and style)	3	3	0
Working conditions	1	5	0
Company policy and supervision (guidelines)	1	3	2
Pay system	0	2	4

Figure 6: Evaluation of organisational surveys in terms of actions (Sample: 10 German companies)

In an overall evaluation, most survey project leaders expressed their satisfaction with the final results of the surveys. At the same time, they stressed the point that further improvements in the management of surveys were possible and necessary.

b) Overcoming superiors' resistance to surveys

One of the main arguments was that the effficiency of surveys is negatively influenced by the existing resistance of superiors. Figure 7 shows what could be done from the point of view of survey project managers to overcome superiors' resistance.

Overcoming superiors' resistance to surveys by ..	Experts' rating		
	very effective	effective	less effective
Information:	7	1	1
strong top management support:	6	2	1
individual consulting:	4	4	1
participation	3	5	1
strong survey-manager support:	3	2	3
protection against negative consequences:	2	2	3
implementing and improving survey in small steps:	1	3	4
support for survey as part of performance evaluation:		1	6

Figure 7: Main determinants of overcoming superiors' resistance to surveys (Sample: 10 German companies)

The most significant factors were more and better information of the superiors and stronger top management support mentioned.

c) Workers' evaluation of organisational surveys

The question how do workers evaluate organisational surveys was beyond the scope of the present research. However, the experts were asked to give an importance-rating of determinants which might influence workers' evaluation in a positive or negative way.

Workers' evaluation of survey-induced actions is influenced by...	Importance-rating		
	very important	important	less important
INFORMATION			
about Survey-results:	10		
about Survey-induced actions:	10		
about restrictions in decision-making:	6	3	1
from management and from immediate superiors:	6	3	1
PARTICIPATION			
in analysis of Survey-results:	4	1	5
in action planning:	4	4	2

Figure 8: Importance-rating of determinants influencing workers' evaluation of survey-induced actions (Sample: 10 German companies)

It is interesting to notice that the workers' perception and evaluation of OS-induced action programmes were strongly influenced by the information received and the possibility to participate in the process of turning OS-results into action.

Figure 8 supports the idea that information is even more important for the workers than participation.

Case Studies in Organisational Surveys' Applications

The application of organisational surveys was studied in four different German organisations (A-D). The types of reactions observed are shown below.

Types of Reactions	A M	A W	B M	B W	C M	C W	D M	D W
Refusing OS		o	o		o			
Denying results	o							
Justifying results	o							
Allocating results	o		o	o	o	o		
Coping through constructive improvement	o	▼					o	o
Actions Programmes	Yes		No		No		Yes	
Promoter of OS	University Institute		Head-quarters		Head-quarters		Workers' Council Management	

A: Construction Machinery   M: Management
B: Telecommunication   W: Workers
C: Household Applicances   Council
D: Chamber of Small Trade

Our conclusions are:

1. There is no one best way for managing organisational surveys. Instead of looking for the optimal approach, research should elaborate approaches which will fit the specific situation of the organisation in which the survey is conducted.

2. Overcoming superiors' resistance to surveys is one of the most critical factors if the efficiency of surveys is to be improved in the future. Some recommendations on what to do can be drawn from the present findings.

3. Organisational surveys will show their true importance as a management tool only if they are repeated in carefully planned periods of time. The management of surveys will then be able to provide the opportunity to learn from success and failure. Survey management should change whenever the situative conditions change, but rather in small steps than in dramatic breaks with past practices.

References

Ackermann, K.-F.: Computergestützte Motivations - und Zufriedenheits-forschung als Instrument der betrieblichen Personalpolitik, in: Brauer, W. (Hrsg.), Informatik-Fachberichte, Bd. 50, Berlin 1981, pp. 527-541.

Ackermann, K.-F: Mitarbeiterbefragungen als Instrument partizipativer Entlohnungspolitik, in: BFuP, 1/1986.

Beck, M.: Durchführung von Mitarbeiterbefragungen. Erfagrungen in der deutschen Industrie, in: Personalwirtschaft 10. Jg. (1983), H. 2, pp. 40-46.

Domsch, M.: Attitude Surveys and Participative Management, Working Paper, Hamburg 1984.

Loveridge, R.: What is Participation? A Review of the Literature and Some Methodological Problems in: British Journal of Industrial Relations 18/1980, pp. 297-317.

Locke, E.A. and Schweiger, D.M.: Participation in Decision-making: One More Look, in: Staw, B.M., Research in Organisational Behaviour, Greenwich 1979, Vol. I, pp. 265 - 339.

Nadler, D. et al.: The Ongoing Feedback System. Experimenting with a New Managerial Tool, in: Organisational Dynamics, Vol. 4 (1976), pp. 63-80.

Paul, G.: Bedürfnisberücksichtigung durch Mitbestimmung, Diss., München 1977.

Schanz, G.: Immaterielle Mitarbeiterbeteiligung. Ergebnisse einer Erhebung, in: Personalwirtschaft 12/83.

Sirota, D.: Opinion surveys: The results are in, what do we do with them? in: Personnel, 1974.

Starke, F.A. and Ferratt, Th.W.: Behavioural Information Systems, in: Journal of Systems Management, Vol. 27 (1976), Nr. 3, pp. 26-30.

Thierry, Henk: Rewarding Participation (1985), in: BFUP, 1/1986.

Töpfer, A. and Zander, E. (Eds.):
Mitarbeterbefragungen, Frankfurt-New York 1985.

Vogel, A.: Employee Surveys:The Risks, the Benefits,
in: Personnel, Vol. 59 (1982), Nr. 1, S. 65 - 70.

Wächter, H.: Partizipation und Mitbestimmung in der
Krise, in: Staehle, W.H. and Stoll, E. (Hrsg.),
Betriebswirtschaftslehre und ökonomische Krise,
pp. 307 - 319.

Chapter Six

ATTITUDE SURVEYS AS A DIRECT OR INDIRECT MEANS
TOWARDS PARTICIPATIVE MANAGEMENT

M Domsch

Introduction

Participative management is mainly based on two
dimensions (Brose and Corsten 1983; Wall and Lischeron
1977)
1. Intensive cooperation between management and
    employees
2. High power for the employees to influence
    decision-processes
With regard to these two dimensions "cooperation" and
"decision-power" there are different types of
management from the employee's point of view.

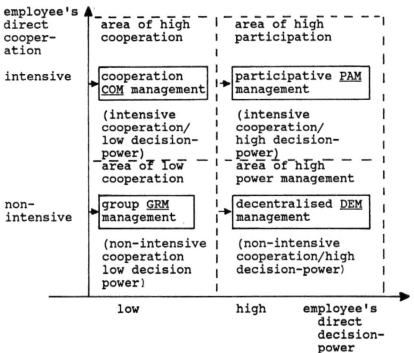

Figure 1: Types of Management

- group management (GRM)

- cooperation management (COM)

- decentralised management (DEM)

- participative management (PAM)

These different types of management are also represented by different personnel management systems instruments or tools etc. (Figure 2). In this paper "attitude surveys" as one "instrument" will be discussed.

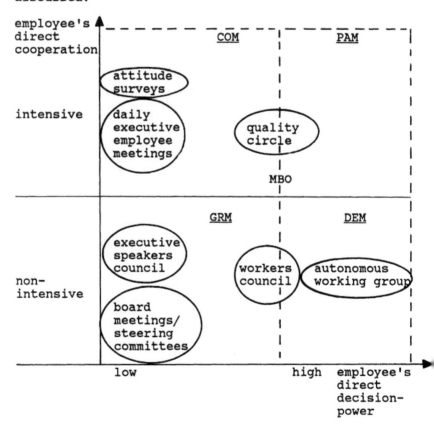

Figure 2: Examples of Personnel Management tools

From the employee's point of view there are two important disadvantages to the more traditional approaches to participation.

1. Indirect participation - When participative management devices such as workers' councils, steering committees, board meetings etc. are used the direct participation of employees is extremely limited.

2. Selective participation - It can not be taken for granted that those employees participating in collaborative efforts are true representatives of all company employees.

"Attitude Surveys", as a special tool of cooperation management, would not have these disadvantages. They typically have the following characteristics: they are instruments of cooperation management; used to diagnose employees' attitudes and objectives by anonymous interviewing of all employees concerned using standardised questionnaires (Domsch and Reinecke, 1982).

These traditional attitude surveys are more marketing instruments, special information gathering and diagnostic systems, with extremely low direct decision-power for the employees. They belong to the group of organisational surveys (Conrad and Sydow, 1984).

This chapter addresses the following three questions:

1. What about employee attitude surveys in practice?

2. Why are traditional attitude surveys of the type mentioned above not suitable enough for participative management?

3. What has to be done - especially with regard to decision-power - to change "employee attitude surveys" from being a tool of cooperation management towards a special tool of participative management?

Employee Attitude Surveys in Practice

Concepts and types of employee attitude surveys

Employee attitude surveys on job satisfaction, individual objectives and motives or on other special questions have been known and common for a long time. They belong to the standard set of instruments of empirical social research, in particular of employment

research.   They   can   be   subdivided   roughly   into
attitude surveys comprising a group of enterprises and
attitude   surveys   of   a   single   enterprise   (Büschges
1975, Topfer 1984).

With regard to the type of surveys we can make a broad
distinction between those which are written or oral
(including surveys or surveys by telephone) and those
using an anonymous/open approach.

With respect to the arrangement of questionnaires we
can make a distinction between the type of question
asked (direct - indirect survey), the question format
(open - closed questions) and the type and extent of
standardisation in the catalogue of questions.

These   possibilities   of   differentiation   and
organisation correspond to those which are well-known
in   empirical   social   research,   especially   market
research (Holm 1979). Almost all the different types
can be empirically substantiated by practical examples
taken   from   a   firm's   internal   employee   attitude
surveys.   In   practice,   however,   the   written   and
anonymous form of structured and standardised surveys
with closed and partially open questions has become
generally accepted.   Ultimately, the chosen type is
predominantly dependent upon the objective and the
operationalisation of the survey.

The same applies to the questionnaire contents, that
is what is asked in the survey.   In the following
section some German internal employee attitude surveys
are listed as examples without being described in
detail.

1.   Comprehensive employee attitude surveys.   These
      surveys focus on a variety of different problem
      areas   such   as: job   situation,   information,
      management, training and follow-on training, etc.
      (Beck 1983)   They were used in a number of well-
      known West German firms, for example:

      - Bayerische Hypotheken - und Wechsel-Bank AG
      - Bertelsmann AG
      - Deutsche Shell AG
      - 3 M Deutschland GmbH
      - Esso AG
      - F. Pieroth Weingut Weinkellerei GmbH
      - Hamburg-Mannheimer   Versicherungs-AG   and
        Sachversicherungs-AG
      - IBM Deutschland GmbH

- Karstadt AG
- SCS Scientific Control Systems GmbH

2. Special employee attitude surveys for determining training and follow-on training needs (Leiter 1982, Verheyen and Olivas 1980)

   - B.A.T. Cigaretten-Fabrik GmbH
   - Enka Glanzstoff AG
   - Henkel & Co GmbH
   - Siemens AG

3. Special employee attitude surveys concerning the superior-employee relationship and the election of superiors (Reinecke 1983)

   - Beiersdorf AG
   - Bundersministerium für Wirtschaft
   - Esso AG
   - Hamburger Elektrizitatswerke AG
   - Hauni-Werke Korber & Co. KG
   - Porst Gruppe

4. Special employee attitude surveys concerning career planning and mobility (Domsch and Reinecke 1982, Hoelemann 1976).

   - Deutsche Shell AG
   - Dresdner Bank AG
   - Enka Glanzstoff AG

   Results usually have been published in internal reports and company journals, for example the Esso Report, November 1980 (Holm 1982).

The concept of the German "employee attitude survey" working group

The German "Employee Attitude Survey" Working Group was established in 1978. As at 1984, it includes representatives from the following enterprises:

- BASF AG
- Bertelsmann AG
- 3 M Company Deutschland GmbH
- Esso AG
- Hamburg-Mannheimer Versicherungs-AG
- IBM Deutschland GmbH
- Karstadt AG
- Vorwerk & Co. as well as the author of this article.

The working group has submitted a concept for general comprehensive employee attitude surveys. It includes: Objectives, Project Planning/Process Management Plan (Figure 3) and a Standard Questionnaire (Domsch 1980). The following key areas are being addressed in this questionnaire:

Place of work	3 questions
Job situation	8 questions
Information	3 questions
Follow-on training and development	4 questions
Management	16 questions
Cooperation/ coordination	4 questions
Income and fringe benefits	5 questions
Image of the enterprise	3 questions
Loyalty to the enterprise	2 questions
Statistics	2 questions
Open questions	1 question.

The list indicates that the questions predominantly relate to the employees' jobs where they touch on complexes which directly address employee interests. The approach, therefore, is based on immediate personal involvement.

It will be often necessary to provide a more detailed analysis of specific problem areas subsequently, since the attitude survey can often only furnish initial indications.

This questionnaire has been repeatedly reviewed methodologically and tested empirically. It has already been employed in a considerable number of surveys, for example of Sonopress (Bertelsmann AG) personnel, the F. Pieroth Weingut Weinkellerei GmbH, the Karstadt AG, 3M Company and the Esso AG.

Following the publication of the concept of the German Working Group, up to now, more than 1,600 companies/institutes of different size, legal form, affiliation to a branch of industry etc. have expressed their interest in additional and feedback information on the subject. This is at least an indication that in practice this subject is dealt with or intended to be dealt with in more detail. Thus, the schedule for 1985 of the "Employee Attitude Survey Working Group" included:

1. The establishment of discussion and feedback groups (including evaluation going beyond single firms and comparisons of enterprises on the basis of survey results).

2. The concept of a human resource-oriented early-warning system including employee attitude surveys.

3. The integration of more special employee attitude surveys into a concept of participative management.

<u>Suitability of attitude surveys for participative management</u>

In principal employees have two ways to increase their power in company decision processes (Figure 4):

- a direct approach: COM > PAM and an indirect/representative approach: COM > GRM > PAM

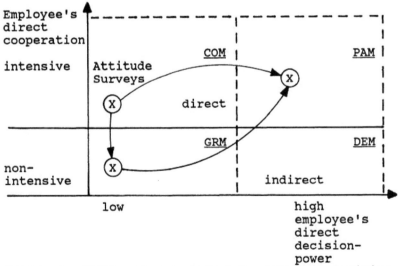

Figure 4: Different approaches to get more decision-power

Analysing the indirect approach in detail results in the identification of the following assumptions of this approach.

The assumption of an unfiltered flow of information

It is possible to maintain a direct dialogue between individual employees or groups and management independently of the management hierarchy by means of personal letters, discussions in employees' meetings, newsletters and information booklets, articles in company magazines and similar devices.

Due to lack of time and funds, this can usually be achieved in individual cases only, not at regular intervals. Therefore, the individual employee is forced to pursue his interests through a multi-stage double hierarchy: through executives in the management hierarchy and through the hierarchy of elected representatives of interests (hierarchy of representation), i.e. the works councils, union representatives, or speakers' committees.

It is, however, unrealistic to assume that the respective flow of information - top down or bottom up - is unfiltered. It has been repeatedly pointed out that senders and recipients of information are affected by transfer, selection and interpretation errors as well as time delays. The larger the number of senders and recipients the higher is the risk of a faulty transfer of information. It is also known that external influences may adversely affect the flow of information in its form, contents, and speed (such as trade unions, employers' associations, public pressure groups etc.).

We are also aware of the role of "gatekeepers". "Gatekeepers" can qualitatively and quantitatively change the information and its flow either consciously or subconsciously by mixing them with other information, especially from their own interests. Gatekeepers for example, can be individual superiors not fulfilling their duties who are modifying flows of information according to their own personal interests. Faults and deficiencies will frequently be veiled in order not to endanger their own position or career. The discussion of personal acceptance or resistance in change situations is also relevant here. (Böhnisch 1979, Suffel 1981). In a project which had been completed and in which among others about 600 executive employees had been interviewed, about 25% of them indicate difficulties with their superiors. In the relations between superiors and employees, and with the next higher superior, one encounters typically rights to hearings of complaints, discussions, and interviews which offer opportunities for the gatekeeper role to be exercised. Finally it has been found that executive employees talk a lot about participation, but they have difficulties in translating it into reality (Marchington 1980).

Groups of superior managers can also distort the information flow. Lately this became apparent in the so-called "AEG case" in which employees and their representatives complained that middle and top AEG management would block and filter information selfishly and/or boycott initiated measures. Works councils or speakers' committees and other representatives may be influential. Those cases are also specified in which elected works councils become independent of or alienated from their clientele (Wilpert 1975, Zündorf and Grant 1980).

Holders of key positions such as secretaries, company secretaries, staff and coordinating agencies can also block the information.

Systems themselves may be inadequate. Information systems may not provide for particular flows of information, and organisational structures, such as a matrix organisation where conflict arises by means of which information can be changed and compromises be effected, are also likely sources of difficulty.

The person himself may be the problem, if he or she suffers from inhibitions or is afraid or incapable of openly attending to his/her interests for reasons of socio-economic status, or language proficiency (Badura 1972, Paul 1977).

Information will then be filtered or modified, canalised, stopped or eventually destroyed. This can lead to efficiency problems and losses of motivation.

The Assumption of Homogeneity of Manpower

Although in practice a hierarchical system of representatives has come to be generally accepted as a parallel hierarchy consisting of works councils and speakers' committees to safeguard and enforce employee interests, in many enterprises not all employees want such a body of representatives. The assumption of homogeneity - relating to the problems of representation - is therefore unrealistic.

In enterprises without a speakers' committee, the executive employees are not represented in a corresponding organisation. If speakers' committees exist, not all executive employees want to be represented by these committees in all matters. As compared with the Labour-Management Relations Act, the rights of the speakers' committees are, in addition, predominantly limited to rights to hearings and consultations.

Part of the other executive employees who are - de jure - represented by the works council, often do not want to be represented de facto, since they rather feel that they belong to management. It is at least dependent upon the situation whether they identify themselves with their representatives in the works council. This split in their feelings with respect to their affiliations also leads to executive employees' demands for more firmly establishing their own representation of interests (Witte, Kallman and Sachs 1980).

When a proportion of the employees do not have management responsibility, they may not think themselves to be represented or, in many cases, do not want to be represented. This relates not only to specialists (EDP experts, safety engineers, commissioners for data privacy protection, corporation lawyers etc.), but also to parts of all employee groups. Indications are furnished by survey results, percentages voting, and the degree of organisation. These arguments can also be documented by results of a survey undertaken by the Deutsche Angestellten Gewerkschaft (German Employees' Union; DAG) on 1,500 works council members from more than one branch of industry: 41% of the works council members who did not want to be renominated as a candidate found their work in the firm "in no way rewarded by their colleagues". 47% of the members rated the employees' interest in the works council activity as being "low" or "nonexistent". 17% of those interviewed found that "their colleagues'" lack of understanding for the works council activities was a special burden. (Dag 1980). In a survey undertaken by the trade union for the printing and paper industry in 1980, 56% of the members stated that they would like to be included in the information chain and in the discussions when enforcing their interests against management. Surveys of the industrial trade union for the metal industry have shown that 23% of the workers and employees interviewed assessed the works council activity as being "less successful" and as "unsuccessful". In the last employee attitude survey of a petroleum company, 30.1% of the 3,200 interviewees, when asked "Do you think that your personal interests are well taken care of by the works council?" answered "No, I don't think so in most cases" and 12.5% of them with "No, not at all". It must, however, be pointed out that the majority of the interviewees expressed a positive point of view. We also accept that these statements cannot be generalised since no representative studies had been undertaken, although the German Trade Union's federation have declared that they should be conducted.

What matters is generally the "support" (percentage of votes in the works council election, negotiating power of the general works council, attendance at the workers' meeting) afforded the employees' representations by the personnel. (Witte 1980).

In the political sector, however, the phenomenon of apathy is emphasised which is characterised by "non-participation of the masses". (Scharf 1972, Rolke 1973). The competition of the political interests with other relevant individual interests and the small amount of time which can be spent by the individual in reality would contradict the utopian idea that all citizens would like to participate in all decision processes concerning themselves. If transferred to the company sector, this would emphasise the argument that part of the employees do not want any individual direct participation in the articulation, safeguarding and enforcement of their interests. This may be largely based on indifference caused by the most varied influences. In this connection sociological and sociopsychological studies especially point to the problem of alienation, aloofness, the lack of identification by the employees with the objectives of the enterprise, the organisation, and job content. (Israel 1972, Bergler 1976, Friedel-Howe 1981).

The Assumption of Comprehensive Rights of Representation

It is undisputed today - at least on the employees' side - that the laws, agreements and guidelines mentioned also show deficiencies with regard to the possibility of elucidating and enforcing employees' interests. Employees' representatives in particular are therefore requesting a modification of codetermination laws, an amendment of the Labour-Management Relations Act, the Data Protection Act, and similar regulations. Subjects of discussion are the demands for increased participation rights, for new types of participation, for increased protection of the rights within the statutes of an enterprise, as it is argued that there were already de jure deficiencies in representation.

This line of reasoning has shown that employees' interests in the existing framework of the parallel hierarchy (management hierarchy and hierarchy of representation) are frequently safeguarded only to a limited extent by management. Secondly, the elected bodies representing special interests (de jure or de facto) only represent part of the employees and thus the "employees interests" voiced by them may also concern only part of the entire personnel. Finally, employees' interests can only be exercised and enforced in part by making use of the existing rights of participation, an expansion of which is largely refused on the employers' side.

Within the framework of the comprehensive discussion on "participation", persons engaged in scientific and practical work have made plenty of suggestions to effect an adequate modification. Some literature on participation can only be referenced here· (Brose and Corsten 1983, Bell 1979, Grunwald and Lilge 1979, Kappler 1980, Marchington 1980, Stein and Reisacher 1980). In the following section the emphasis will remain exclusively on the question of the extent to which a firm's internal employee attitude surveys are suited for detecting and enforcing employee interests to reduce the above-mentioned deficiencies in representation.

Employee attitude surveys and decision-power

The phenomenon of power within an enterprise has been investigated by numerous scientists (Kotter 1979, Reber 1980, Schneider 1977). In general, power is any attempt to enforce one's own will in a social relationship even against resistance, no matter what this chance is based on (French and Raven 1959).

Within the scope of this paper we can only focus here on the question whether and to what extent employee attitude surveys can change the distribution of decision-power in the enterprise? This question should be answered if the following points are being considered:

1. Who initiates a firm's internal attitude surveys? One can differentiate here between:

    -   Employer/management or their representatives
    -   Employees or their representatives (such as the works council, speakers' committee)
    -   Management and the works council together.

So far, employee attitude surveys have been mainly initiated by the company's management but recently a shift toward a more interactive creation of survey projects (the third alternative) can be observed.

2. Who will receive the information gathered? Here a rough distinction can be made between only the part ordering the survey and sharing the information with other interest groups.

    If for example management orders the survey, it can also make the information gained available to the works council and all employees concerned through a firm's internal channel of information. Additional differentiations result if the user selects the information, or adds interpretations.

3. To what extent does the recipient want to and can he employ the results of the employee attitude survey to influence the decision processes directly or indirectly? Here, all degrees of cooperation and participation known can be realised. The following are considered to be characteristic examples:

-   In the course of hearings, individual employees, groups or selected employee representatives substantiate the requirement for the fulfilment of certain employee interests with the use of results from employee attitude surveys.

-   Management employs survey results to state the reasons why it can or cannot or wants or does not want to fulfil certain requirements.

-   Survey results are included in consultations on planning measures.

- Employees/employees' representatives and/or
  employers/employer's representatives base their
  planning and decision-making on the survey
  results.

- No planning may be undertaken and/or decisions be
  made if a majority (or a certain percentage) of
  those interviewed in employee attitude surveys
  state that this opposes their interests.

On the basis of three examples it is briefly shown
which shifts may ensue in the distribution of power
(Figure 5).

This consideration shows that considerable shifts in
the distribution of decision-power may occur. In
general, the following relationships hold true:

The stronger the obligation to attend to employees
interests which is derived from the results of
employee attitude surveys, the

- greater the increase in power for the employees'
  interest group in case of harmony,

- greater the decrease in power for the employees'
  representatives in case of conflict,

- greater the increase in power for the employees'
  representatives in case of harmony,

- greater the decrease in power for the employee
  interest group/management in case of conflict.

Seen realistically, the employee interest group may -
if only for a short time - be distinguished from the
employees' representations when employee attitude
surveys are employed. For the elected representatives
will not, in the long run, reject employee interest
voiced in attitude surveys - if any differences become
apparent at all. If we only differentiate between
employees' and employers' interest groups, employee
attitude surveys will tend in the described cases to
increase employee' decision-power and decrease the
decision-power of the employers.

In summary:

- The more obligation towards the results coming out of employee attitude surveys, the higher is the decision-power for employees;

- the more participative is a company's management approach.

It has become obvious in discussions and hearings conducted by the German Working Group on Employee Attitude Surveys that there will be opposition to employee attitude surveys if direct rights of participation can be derived from the results and, thus, the above-mentioned shifts of power may occur.

On the one hand, such opposition is to be expected from trade unions/works councils since they refer to their rights of representation which they are legally entitled to and to the fact that they would represent the interests of their voters (employees) as a matter of course.

On the employers' side a shift of power to the capital owners' disadvantage is being more or less globally rejected to an increasing extent - irrespective of the subject matter under discussion. This is shown by the discussion about the codetermination laws, but also the amendment of the Labour-Management Relations Act, the Data Protection Act etc.

A major part of the executives will, although they themselves belong to the group of employees, also oppose a restriction of the latitude in decision-making they have been allowed so far. On the one hand, their argument rests on the requirement for more extensive specialised knowledge, on the other hand, it is pointed out that the superior's obligation to attend to the welfare of his employees also imposes upon him the task of attending to their interests.

Representatives of different sciences argue that direct personal participation of all employees in decision-making processes is a kind of utopian ideal for all fundamental attitude in social theory which is, however, unrealistic.

Seen from this perspective, it should be realistic to recognise that in the foreseeable future employee attitude surveys do not have a chance of being accepted as a de jure instrument of participative

management.   But following the present discussion
about this area it seems to be realistic to expect
special employee attitude surveys to have direct
influence upon decision-processes. From this point of
view there may be a good chance that these surveys can
be used as a special tool for particular questions and
problems   within   the   realms   of   participative
management.

References

Badura, B: Befürfnisstruktur und Politisches System.
Macht, Kultur und Kommunikation in Pluralitischen
Gesellschaften. Stuttgart 1972.

Beck, M: Durchführrung von Mitarbeiterbefragungen.
Erfahrungen in der Deutschen Industrie, in
Personalwirtschaft 1983 pp 40-46.

Bell, W D: Industrial Participation. London 1979.

Bergler, R: Welche Bebeutung had die wachsende distanz
zwischen führenden und geführten für die
willensbildung im unternehmen? In Albach H und
Dadowski D (Eds). Die Bedeutung Gesellschaft.

Böhnish, W: Personale Widerstande bei der Durchbetzung
von innovationen, Stuttgart 1979.

Brose P, and Corsten H: Partizipation in der
Unternehmung München 1983 (pp 13-15).

Büschges, C: Betriesumfragen in: Gaugler, E
Handwörterbuch des Personalwesens Stuttgart 1975
(pp 699-704).

Conrad, P and Sydow, J: Organisationsklima. Frankfurt
and New York 1984 DAG Deutsche Angesttelten -
gewerkschaft, landesverband. Hamburg (editors):
Betriebsver-fassung und betriebsrats-arbeit aus
der sicht Hamburger Betriebsrats-mitglieder.
Ergebnisse einer umfrage der dag-Hamburg zur
arbeit als betriebsratsmitglied. Hamburg 1980.

Domsch, M and Mitarbeiterbegragungen als REINECKE
fürungsinstrument in: Schuler, Heinz und Stehle W:
Psychologie in Wirtschaft und Verwaltung.
Stuttgart 1982. pp 127-148.

Domsch, M and Reinecke, P: Partizipative Personalent-
wicklung in Kossbiel H (HRG). Personal-
entwicklung, Sonderheft nr 14 der zeitschrfit für b
etriebswirtswirtschaft-liche forschung Wiesdbaden
1982
(pp 64-81).

Domsch, M: Mitarbeiterbefragungen Interview und
Analyse Vol 7 1980 (pp 419-443).

French, J R P and Raven, B: The Bases of Social Power.
In Cartwright D (Ed) Studies in Social Power Ann
Arbor 1959 (pp 150-167).

Friedel-Howe, H: Entfremdung in der Industriearbeit.
Ansatz eines sozialisations-theoretischen
besugsrahmens der psychischen vermittlung
situativer entfremdungs-potentiale. Berlin 1981.

Grunwald, W and Lilge, H G: Partizpative fürhung,
(eds) betriebswirtschafliche und sozial
psychologische aspect. Bern und Stuttgart 1980.

Holemann, W: Laufbahnplanung für führungskrafte in
zeitschrift für betriebswirtschaftliche forschung-
kontaltstudium. Vol 28 1976 (pp 105-113).

Holm, K: (HRG) Die befragung. Band 1.6 München 1975-
1979.

Holm, K F: Die Mitarbeiterbefragung. Hamburg 1982.

Israel, J: Der Begriff der Entremdung Makrosozio-
logische unter-suchung von Marx bis zur soziologie
der gegenwart. Reinbek Hamburg 1972.

Kappler, E: "Partizipation" in Grochla E (Ed).
Handwörterbuch der Organisation, 2nd Edition.
Stuttgart 1980. (pp 1845-1855).

Kotter, J P: Power in Management New York 1979.

Leiter, R et al: Der weiterbildungsbedarf im
Unternehmen. Method der ermittlung. München und
Wien 1982 pp 83-134.

Marchington, M: Problems with Participation at Work.
Personnel Review Vol. 9 No 3. 1980. (pp31-38).

Marchington, M: Responses to Participation at Work.
Westmead. Farnborough 1980.

Paul, G: Bedürfnisberücksichtigung durch Mitestimmung.
München 1977 (pp 160 FF).

Reber, G: (HRSG) Macht in Organisationen. Stuttgart
1980.

Reinecke, P: Vorgesetztenbeurteilung. Ein Instrument
Partizipativer führung und Organisation-
sentwicklung. Köln 1983.

Rölke, P: Die Boteiligung von Gewerkschaftsmitgliedern
    der unteren organisationseben an der
    innergewerkschaftlichen willensbildung.
    Dissertation. Köln 1973.

Scarpf, F W: Demokratietheorie zwischen Utopie und
    Anpassung. 2nd edition. Konstanz 1972.

Schneider, H D: Sozial Psychologie der machtbeziehunge
    n Stuttgart 1977.

Stein, E. and Reisacher, E: (Eds)   Mitbestimmung über
    den arbeitzsplatz   Köln 1980.

Suffel, W: Widerstand von Geschäft-bereichsleitern im
    entwicklungsprozess der strategischen planung.
    Frankfurt 1981.

Töpfer, A: Mitarbeiterbefragungen. In: Managementenz-
    Klopädie 2 auflage, Landsberg am lech 1984 pp 892-
    911.

Verheyen, L G and Olivas, L: Attitude survey supports
    training needs.   Public Personnel Management. Vol
    9 1980 (pp 31-35).

Wall, T D and Lischeron, J A: Worker Participation.
    London 1977 pp 36-46.

White, M: Getting the drift of employee attitudes.
    Personnel Management Vol 10 1980   pp38-42.

Wilpert, B: Research of Industrial Democracy.   The
    German Case.   Industrial relations Journal.   Vol 6
    1975 (pp 53-64).

Witte, E, Kallman, A and Sachs G: Führungskräfte als
    zukünftiges problemfeld, zeitschrift für
    organisation Vol 49 No 1.   1980 (pp 13-19).

Witte, E: Das einflusspotential der arbeitnehmer als
    grundlage der mitBestimmung, die
    BetrieBswirtschaft vol 40.   1980.   (pp3-26).

Zündorf, L and Grunt M: Hierarchie in Wirtschafts-
    unternehmen.   Die sozialen beziehungen zwischen
    vorgesetzen und ihren untergebenen in industrie
    und dienstleistungsunternehmen.   Frankfurt and New
    York 1980.

Chapter Seven

MEASURING THE QUALITY OF WORKING LIFE, USING
INSTITUTIONAL AND QUESTIONNAIRE APPROACHES

J Soeters and F Nijhuis

Introduction

In the comparative analysis of organisations survey
research is predominant. Generally speaking, such
surveys are based on either of two methods of data
collection. The first method is the so-called
questionnaire approach. In this method responses of
non-biased samples or organisation members are
aggregated to obtain measures of organisational
characteristics (Ven and Ferry, 1980). The questions
frequently are at the level of the individual's job.
The other approach is the institutional method. In
this case the measures may be of two types. In its
"rigid" form this method relies on organisational
charts and documents, and consequently the measures
focus on organisational practices that can be observed
objectively. A second form of the institutional
method may be a questionnaire administered at the top-
level of the organisation. In this way, chief
executive officers may be asked their opinions of
various organisational practices. These responses
regard parts of the organisation as a whole; they may
then be interpreted as institutional measures. Both
types of institutional measures have been made popular
by the Aston research programme (Pugh et al., 1968).

It is often claimed (Pennings, 1973), that both
methods - the institutional and the questionnaire
approach - measure the same organisational
characteristics. This raises the empirical question,
to what extent can convergence be observed between
these two methods of data collection? This question
is of more than mere academic importance.

It is said, that each approach has its theoretical and
practical weaknesses (Sathe, 1978). For example the
questionnaire approach may be criticised for
generating "subjective" information. Furthermore,

this method has to deal with difficult aggregation problems (Walton, 1981). Thirdly, it is not as economical as the institutional approach. Due perhaps to this last property, the institutional method seems to be more popular, especially with regard to the measurement of organisational structure (Pugh and Hickson, 1976; Khandwalla, 1977; Lammers and Hickson, 1979; Koot, 1980).

The reason for this relative popularity seems logical. The institutional method is practical, easily manageable and less expensive than observations amongst samples of employees. One may, however, seriously question whether this popularity is justified. The weaknesses of the institutional approach may be even more evident than its practical advantages. In general, critics point to the fact that the definition of many variables in organisational surveys has not always had one and the same meaning for everybody involved. This creates at least two problems. Firstly, while responding to the questions, the key-informants use their own frame of reference. In other words they give their own definitions of the "situation" and their own cognitive and perceptual "maps". Since the key-respondents normally occupy positions at the top of the organisation, the responses may therefore be criticised for their lack of ideological neutrality (Nichols, 1969; Koot, 1980). Secondly, as a consequence of limitations in internal communication and information-structure in an organisation it may be that the key spokesmen do not know all the answers to the questions. If this lack of knowledge is not taken into account (for example with respect to aspects of the informal organisation), serious errors in measurement may result (Nijhuis, 1984).

Despite these shortcomings the institutional method is quite popular with scholars studying organisation structure. However, in the field of the quality of working life these methodological disadvantages seem to weigh more heavily. The "ideology" factor is considered to be especially important, and therefore the institutional method is seldom used in this area of investigation, (Lawler, 1975; Quinn and Staines, 1978; Seashore, 1981). In "quality of working life" investigations it is the perception of employees that is nearly always measured. As such, the questionnaire approach is predominant in this area of investigation.

Nevertheless, as mentioned before, the two methods of data collection are said to measure the same organisational characteristics. It is pertinent to ask, therefore, if this can be shown to be true with regard to the measurement of the quality of working life. This is important because, if so, the institutional method could very well be applied to this area of investigation. If, on the other hand, it could be shown that the two methods cannot be used interchangeably, the use of the institutional method in measuring the quality of working life may be in doubt.

For this reason, some empirical results concerning the convergence between these two methods of data collection will be presented in this paper. The data consists of 51 industrial and non-industrial organisations in the Netherlands.

Prior research on the comparison of the institutional and questionnaire approach

Pennings (1973) was the first to pay attention to the question of convergence between the two methods of data collection. He tried to answer this question on the basis of data from 10 business organisations. He concentrated on the measurement of centralisation and formalisation, both being aspects of organisation structure. He used "classical" instruments of the institutional and questionnaire approach. As far as the questionnaire was concerned, it turned out that the overall response rate was close to 50%. Although this response rate may be judged as rather low, Pennings did not see this as a serious problem.

The results of his study were not very satisfactory. The measure of the two methods appeared to correlate only slightly or even negatively. Unidimensionality of the components could therefore not be observed. The provisional conclusion had to be that the two methods of data-collection relate to different aspects of organisation structure.

Lammers (1983) comes to the same conclusion. On examining Pennings' findings, his opinion is that the institutional method measures the official or formal characteristics of the organisation whereas the questionnaire approach expresses the factual day-to-day reality in organisational life. According to Lammers and Hickson (1979), the two methods express the distinction between organisational form and organisational régime, respectively between the "anatomy" and the "physiology" of organisations. With this interpretation Lammers and Hickson point to the same specific properties of the institutional method as was mentioned earlier in this paper. Key informants are not always aware of everything happening in the organisation, especially, with regard to the informal aspects of behaviour.

There is other research that points to the conclusion that the two methods do not measure the same organisational dimensions. Sathe (1978) investigated the same problem as Pennings, concentrating on the same organisational concepts: formalisation and centralisation. His response rate in the questionnaire approach was 66%. In contrast to Pennings, he controlled for organisational size, while comparing the measures of the two methods. Again the measurements of the institutional and questionniare approach showed low convergence. In his conclusion Sathe indicates that institutional measures generally tap the formal or designed structure whereas the questionnaire measures describe the emergent (day-to-day) experienced structure. This interpretation is found to be similar to Lammers' conclusion concerning the Pennings' findings.

Finally, Ford (1979) made another attempt to examine the question. He used data concerning 68 departments from 8 different organizations. With respect to the questionnaire measures, his response rate was not mentioned. While comparing both the methods, he controlled statistically for organisational size, technology and environment. He concluded that in spite of controlling for context factors, there still on average little convergence, and that caution was needed in making comparisons between studies using the two different approaches.

Thus, examining the findings in this field, it can reasonably be assumed, that the two methods cannot be used interchangeably. Therefore the following general hypothesis was formulated for our investigation:

The convergence between the institutional and questionnaire measures of organisations will be rather low, even if controlled for context factors.

However, it was decided to reformulate the hypothesis further in this paper. As pointed out earlier, the institutional method is the most often used. It is applied not only in fundamental research, but also in pragmatic or applied organisational research. Mostly, in this latter kind of research, the research is for indicators, that can statistically explain a major part of the variance of a dependent variable. Examples are Dutch "institutional" studies, which aim at finding organisational characteristics that can explain the difference in average absenteeism between companies (e.g. Philipsen, 1969; Nijhuis and Soeters, 1982; Smulders, 1984). With reference to the afore-mentioned discussion, one may speculate which of the two methods of data collection is more fruitful in explaining the variance of any given phenomenon at the organisational level.

Again, this is an important question. If the institutional method was found to have less power in explaining results than the questionnaire approach, this would imply that this method does not deserve its current popularity.

In this regard it is argued that the questionnaire approach expresses the factual, emergent and not the designed organisation. Consequently the reformulated hypothesis is:

Data, collected by the questionnaire approach, are more powerful in explaining organisational phenomena.

This hypothesis will be tested with respect to absenteeism. In studying the quality of working life, absenteeism is a very "logical" dependent variable (Philipsen, 1969; Gardell, 1975; Smulders, 1984; Steers and Rhodes, 1984).

Research-design and instruments

In 1981 a large research project was commenced with two colleagues. This project was aimed at detecting causes of absenteeism at the organisational level. In this research project the two methods of data collection were used. For the institutional approach, the research-procedures, as applied by Philipsen in 1969 were followed. His method implied measurement of organisational characteristics on the basis of interviews with the Chief Executive Officer and the Personnel Manager. For the questionnaire method, samples of employees of each participating organisation were interviewed concerning their work and performance. Consequently, both the institutional and questionnaire method were used collecting similar information at different levels within the same organisation.

The reason why both approaches were followed is of a political nature. This research project was carried out with the financial support of the Dutch government, and what could be described as a supervisory committee was established. In this committee, both employers' organisations and labour unions were represented amongst others. The representatives of the labour unions objected to the preliminary research design, consisting of using only the institutional method. In their view this would have led to an employers' view on the subject. In fact, they then expressed the same criticism of the ideologically non-neutral character of the institutional measures, as has been put forward earlier (Nichols, 1969; Koot, 1980).

Even an adaptation of the original design (not only interviews with Management and the personnel department, but also with a delegation of the Work's Council) in their view was not satisfactory. The resistance of the labour unions to the institutional research design became so strong, that the University of Limburg offered additional financial support. This enabled a questionnaire research project to be carried out among samples of employees. The combination of this questionnaire investigation and the adapted version of the institutional design, was finally agreed upon by all members of the supervising committee. A unique research project could then begin.

Thus, the project consisted of two parts:

i) an investigation by means of interviews with key spokesmen at the top of the organisation (Nijhuis and Soeters, 1982);

ii) a questionnaire investigation among the personnel of the organisations participating (Schroer et al., 1984).

With respect to both parts there follows a brief description of sampling procedures, and response rate.

i) The sampling population of this part of the investigation was all organisations in South Limburg (the most southerly part of the Netherlands) having at least 50 employees. From this population a total of 99 organisations were approached with the request to participate in this investigation. Finally, 51 organisations, equally distributed in all branches of the population (including governmental organisations) agreed to participate. As mentioned already interviews were held with a delegation of the Work's Council. The interviews were held by the two authors of this paper (for information concerning response rate etc, see Nijhuis and Soeters, 1982).

ii) Next, a select sample of employees was drawn, with the personnel lists of the 51 participating organisations serving as a population. These employees were approached and interviewed at home. In the sampling procedure no category of personnel was excluded. Foreign employees, who were not able to understand and speak the Dutch language, were interviewed with the help of interpreters.

These interviews were distributed over the 51 organisations, in accordance with the number of employees per organisation. One exception was made to this procedure: to increase the reliability, it was decided, that at least 10 employees from each organisation had to be interviewed. Thus, in the case of the smallest participating organisation 20% (i.e. 10 out of 50 employees) were interviewed. In the case of the largest participating organisations (1012 employees) some 8% of all personnel were interviewed.

In this way 1287 employees were approached at home. From this number 1002 employees (= 83%) have in fact cooperated. This response rate may be considered as high, especially in comparison with the results of Pennings (50%) and Sathe (66%) in this regard. The representativeness of the interviewed employees is therefore virtually guaranteed. This was tested by portioning the sample with respect to age, nationality and job level (Schrober et al. 1984). Of course, the smaller organisations have been somewhat oversampled as a consequence of the sampling procedure used.

In both parts of the research project a large number of variables were measured and constructed. (See Nijhuis and Soeters, 1982 and Schroer et al., 1984). All these variables were selected and operationalised in the tradition of the Dutch absenteeism studies, starting with Philipsen (1969). In this tradition and in the previous studies (Nijhuis and Soeters, 1982; Schroer et al., 1984) these variables have been shown to have a satisfying degree of both construct and predictive validity especially with regard to absenteeism (e.g. de Groot, 1975).

In line with other criteria for quality of working life studies one or two constructs were selected for the major conceptual categories of quality of working life (e.g. Walton, 1975) (Figure 1). These variables represent different aspects of the quality of working life. (QWL).

Major category QWL	Research-construct
1. Opportunity for continued growth and security	1. Job security
2. Safe and healthy working conditions	2. Physical working conditions
3/4. Immediate opportunity to use and develop human capacities	3. Socio-psychological working conditions
	4. Participation of employees in decision-making
5. Social integration in the work organisation	5. Activities of personnel management
6. Work and the total life space	6. Irregular work schedules

Figure 1. The QWL research variables.

In order to test the two hypotheses, there was an investigation carried out in both data files for operationalisations which were either conceptually similar or if possible, identical. A total of six variables in both research projects turned out to be comparable. Now there follows a brief discussion of these 2 x 6 variables. All twelve variables have been developed on the basis of factor analysis. All alpha values, indicating the reliability of the measurements, are satisfactory (i.e. $\geq$ 50, see Nunnally, 1967).

MEASURING THE QUALITY OF WORKING LIFE

1. Job security

Threat of unemployment may cause severe distress and insecurity to the future of the employees. It may also lead to a disturbance in the organisational climate.

In the institutional research project this variable was constructed from the answers of the personnel officer, concerning the following questions:

What are the employment prospects in your organisation?

Have there been any collective dismissals in the last three years in your organisation?

What group of the personnel experiences any discomfort about job security?

In this variable job insecurity was measured by inquiring into the employment situation in both the past and in the future. Both these views are highly correlated with one another. Therefore they would be integrated in this construct [alpha for this scale = 0.74].

In the questionnaire-method the individual employees were asked:

Is there a threat of dismissals in your department for the next year?

Do you have enough job security? [alpha for this scale = 0.58].

Evaluating the character of these questions in the two research projects, it may be said that the operationalisation of these two variables is very similar.

2. Physical working conditions

This variable measures the discomfort which the employees experience from the physical working conditions. These conditions are an important determinant of sickness absenteeism.

In the institutional method the personnel officer was asked: "How much discomfort do the employees experience from ....?" followed by 15 different aspects in working conditions, e.g.: noise, dust and temperature. Each of these conditions was given a separate score, differentiated for the two main categories of personnel [alpha for this scale = 0.91]. The questionnaire approach asked the individual workers: "Do you experience any discomfort of ....?", followed by the same 15 working conditions [alpha for this scale = 0.90].

Thus, the operationalisations of these variables are completely identical for the two methods of measurement.

3. Socio-psychological working conditions

The socio-psychological working conditions show the extent to which employees have the opportunity to use their capacities in a good working climate.

The same questions were asked with respect to these socio-psychological working conditions in both the questionnaire and institutional method; the latter responses were supplied by the Personnel Officer. In this variable five aspects such as role ambiguity, working climate, and mental work load were included. Again, these variables may be considered as identically operationalised [alphas for these scales are respectively 0.79 and 0.69].

4. Participation of employees in decision-making on the shop floor

Employees can also develop and use their capabilities through participation in decision-making.

In the institutional part of the project the structure and regularity of employee participation was examined. Questions were asked regarding this subject both of the personnel officer as well as of the delegation of the Works' Council [alpha=0.70]. In the questionnaire approach, the individual employees indicated the level of involvement in decision-making with regard to changes in their work environment [alpha=0.71]. These variables were therefore operationalised in a similar, but, not identical way.

5. Activities of Personnel Management

Since work, sickness and career were considered within the framework of the total organisation, it was important to find out how the organisation gave support to the employees.

In the institutional approach the following questions was asked:

Is there a separate department for Personnel Management?

Does this department have clear job descriptions?

Do the employees of that department have a specialised educational background in Personnel Relations?

Is the Personnel Manager a member of the top management?

These four questions formed the basis for an index "Activities of Personnel Management".

In the questionnaire approach we collected the opinions of the individual employees who were asked:

Can you obtain support, if necessary, from Personnel Management?

Can you obtain support, if necessary, from a Company Social Welfare Officer?

These variables are conceptually similar; the operationalisations, however, are not identical. Both measurements point to the possibility of acquiring professional help, when there are social problems.

6. Irregular Work Schedule

Irregular work schedules, e.g. forms of shift work, may lead to negative effects on other aspects of life. The negative effects will be stronger as the schedules become more intensive. Thus a scale was constructed ranging from low-intensive irregular work schedules to high-intensive irregular work schedules.

Using the institutional approach an index was developed based on the following items:

What section of the employees are working in a two, three, four or five rotation shift system, and

What section of the employees experience discomfort in working a shift system? [alpha for this scale = 0.82].

In the questionnaire approach this variable was represented by an indicator based on the following questions:

Do you work in a shift system?

Do you sometimes work at weekends?

Can you get a day off when you want it?

Do you sometimes have to return to
the organisation on your day off?
[alpha for this scale = 0.59].

We concluded that these variables are operationalised in practice in a similar way.

Comparing the institutional and the questionnaire approach

In this section a comparison between the questionnaire and the institutional variables is undertaken, with the help of a multitrait-multimethod matrix. The multitrait-multimethod approach was first described by Campbell and Fiske (1959). It has also been used by Pennings (1973) for the same research questions as those discussed in this paper. The multitrait-multimethod matrix shows the correlations between the 12 variables (6 questionnaire and 6 institutional variables). These correlations can be classified into three groups:

    i)   Intra-method correlations (multitrait-one method); these are the correlations between the variables, measured by one single method. These groups may be categorized in two sub-groups: the intra-method questionnaire correlations and the intra-method institutional correlations.

    ii)   Intermethod-multitrait correlations (multimethod-multitrait); these are correlations between different variables measured by different methods.

iii) Convergent correlations (one trait-multimethod); these are the correlations between the "identical" or "conceptually similar" variables, measured by different methods. According to Campbell and Fiske (1959), it is possible to speak of a satisfactory convergent validity between two methods, if these correlations are significantly different from zero. To test the first hypothesis special attention was paid to these groups of correlations.

Before presenting the results of the analysis, it is necessary to point to one remaining methodological issue. Preliminary analysis indicated, that the number of employees interviewed in one organisation could be an important factor with regard to the convergence of the two methods (Schröer et al., 1984). Consequently the analysis was carried out for two samples: the total group of organisations (minimal sample-size of interviewed employees in one organisation is 10); [N = 51] and the total group of organisations with at least 200 employees (minimal sample-size in one single organisation is 20); [N = 21].

Results

In the complete multitrait-multimethod correlation matrices of the 12 variables the zero-order correlations were computed as well as the partial correlations. The correlations were also partialized for four context-variables (mean age of the employees, the proportion of female workers, organisational size and industry). In previous research these four variables have been shown to be major organisational determinants of absenteeism. They represent organisational characteristics that are difficult to change (Steers and Rhodes, 1978; Portes and Steers, 1973; Muchinsky, 1977; Chadwick-Jones, Brown and Nicholson, 1973). Therefore, they have to be regarded as contextual variables based on administrative data.

The most important findings of these multitrait-multimethod matrices are presented in Tables 1 and 2. Table 1 presents a summary of the overall characteristics of both matrices. This Table shows: the percentage of significant correlations ($p < 0.05$)

for each different group of correlations and the median (absolute value) correlations of these groups.

Table 1:   A summary of the multitrait-multimethod matrices.

	All organisations (N = 51)		Large organisations (N = 21)	
groups of correlations	% significant correlations	median correlations	% median significant correlations	median correlations
intramethod questionnaire	33 (40)	.16 (.19)	13 (40)	.12 (.31)
correlations intramethod institutional	40 (33)	.15 (.15)	33 (33)	.28 (.27)
correlations intermethod	13 (30)	.12 (.18)	20 (23)	.28 (.25)
multi-trait correlations convergent correlations	83 (83)	.47 (.56)	67 (83)	.47 (.58)

This table indicates, that the group of convergent correlations shows the highest percentage of significant correlations as well as the highest median value. This implies that these findings do not give support to the first hypothesis. The "identical" or "conceptually similar" variables obviously have higher intercorrelations than the other combinations of variables. In contrast, the intermethod-multi-trait correlations are very seldom significant, as might be expected.

The testing of the first hypothesis is continued in Table 2.

Table 2: Convergent correlations between the 2 x 6 "identical" or "conceptually similar" variables.

	(N = 51)		(N = 21)	
Job security	.37**	(.49***)	.79***	(.83***)
Physical working conditions	.57****	(.70***)	.45*	(.72***)
Psycho-social working conditions	.25*	(.17)	.49*	(.29)
Participation in decision-making	.58***	(.62***)	.29	(.49**)
Personnel management	.11	(.52***)	-.13	(.46*)
Irregular Work schedules	.62***	(.64***)	.78***	(.71***)

* : $0.01 < p\ 0.05$ (...) unpartialised
** : $0.001 < p < 0.01$
*** : $p < 0.001$

Table 2 shows that after partialisation five (for N = 51) or four (for N = 21) variables have a significant convergent validity. These variables are:

 job security;
 physical working conditions;
 socio-psychological working conditions;
 participation in decision-making (for N = 51);
 irregular work schedules.

The variable "Personnel Management" shows a strong correlation before partialisation, but after partialisation the size of this correlation diminishes. The most probable explanation of this result may be found in the influence of the size of the organisation. The presence of a separate and structured personnel department strongly depends on the size of the organisation. Thus, the unpartialised correlation shows a strong correlation, which, however, disappears when one controls for organisational size.

Thus, examining the results, the general conclusion must be that in contrast to research by Pennings

(1973), Sathe (1978) and Ford (1979), the first hypothesis must be rejected. In at least four out of six important variables with regard to the measurement of QWL the convergent correlations are satisfactory. This implies that a certain degree of agreement between methods is indeed possible. The presence of convergence between the two methods of data collection is more likely, if the operationalisations are more equal.

The explanatory strength of both methods

The second hypothesis stated that the questionnaire method is more powerful in explaining organisational phenomena than the institutional method. This second hypothesis was tested with regard to patterns of absenteeism (frequency and average duration). These "sick-leave" figures are based on administrative data. The statistical characteristics of these variables are given in Appendix 1.

Table 3 and 4 present the partial correlations between the six questionnaire and six institutional variables and also the variables: frequency of "sick-leave" cases (Table 3) and average duration of "sick-leave" periods (Table 4). A partialisation for the four previously mentioned context variables was carried out. Again the analysis was done separately for the total sample (N = 51) and for the sample of larger organisations (N = 21).

The explained variances given in Tables 3 and 4 are calculated by means of a multiple regression analysis.

Table 3: Partial correlations between the frequency of sickness absenteeism and the comparable questionnaire and institutional variables.

	Frequency of "Sick-leave" cases			
	Total Sample (N = 51)		Large Organisations (N=21)	
	Question-naire variables	Institu-tional variables	Question-naire variables	Institu-tional variables
Security	.26*	-.05	.63**	.63**
Physical working conditions	.11	.35**	.28	.23
Psycho-social working conditions	.18	.40**	.21	.34
Partici-pation	.25*	.24*	.24	.51*
Personnel management	.12	.21	.45*	.30
Irregular work schedule	.10	.03	.14	.26
Multiple R	.33	.47	.66	.66
Multiple R^2	.11	.22	.43	.44

* : $0.01 < p < 0.05$
** : $0.001 < p < 0.01$

On examining the results, it must be remarked that the explained variance is not very high. However, earlier research findings have shown that another set of specific organisational characteristics can explain more than 70% of the "sick-leave" patterns (Nijhuis and Soeters, 1982; see also Philipsen, 1969; Smulders, 1984).

Table 4: Partial correlation between average duration of "sick-leave" periods and the six questionnaire and institutional variables.

	All labour organisations (N = 51)		Larger labour organisations (N=21)	
	Average of "Sick-leave" cases			
	Question-naire variables	Institutional variables	Question-naire variables	Institutional variables
Job security	-.07	-.07	-.02	-.15
Physical working conditions	.24	.17	.02	.35
Psycho-social working conditions	-.14	- .12	-.30	-.05
Partici-pation	-.27*	-.37**	-.08	-.40
Personnel management	.21	-.29*	-.03	-.48*
Irregular work schedule	.17	.15	-.18	-.22
Multiple R	.57	.627	.61	.74
Multiple R^2	.33	.38	.38	.54

* : $0.01 < p < 0.05$
** : $0.001 < p < 0.01$

The findings in Tables 3 and 4 do not give a clear impression regarding the question as to which method is more powerful when explaining organisational phenomena.

It may, however, be concluded that:

i)   In the case of the large sample (N = 51) the
     institutional variables seem to have greater
     explanatory strength than the questionnaire
     variables.

ii) In the sample consisting of only the larger
     organisations the questionnaire approach
     seems to match the institutional approach
     (especially with respect to the "frequency"
     variable).

iii) The variables with sufficient convergent
     correlations have more corresponding
     correlations with frequency and duration
     than the other variables (particularly in
     personnel management).

In conclusion, it may be stated that the evidence
concerning hypothesis two is equivocal and as such
cannot be confirmed by the findings. It is clear that
the questionnaire approach is strongly dependent on
the sample size of the interviewees. When this sample
size is small, the institutional approach appears more
successful.

Discussion

How do these results relate to the findings of
Pennings (1973), Sathe (1978) and Ford (1979)? In
this section an attempt will be made to answer this
question, focusing on three main features.

The operationalisation of concepts

In an evaluation of the above-mentioned studies Walton
(1981) showed in detail, that the operationalisations
of organisational concepts, derived from the
institutional and questionnaire approach, are by no
means identical. At best, the measures of the two
methods are complementary, each focusing on different
aspects of organisational structure. It is therefore
logical, that the two approaches do not converge.
Walton (1981), with this analysis, follows the
conclusions of other researchers, including those of
Lammers (see Section 2), however, Walton goes one step
further.

He points to the fact that normally the questionnaire
measures are descriptions of an individual's job.
They therefore only represent the role of employees.

In his view, aggregated questionnaire measures cannot be taken as a description of organisational features, as long as the items focus on the individual's job. So, he expects to find convergence between the institutional and questionnaire approach if, and only if, the measures of the two methods directly focus on the same level of analysis.

On the basis of the results of the present study it is not possible to agree with the latter part of his argument. These findings show that no convergence between the two methods of data collection occurs if the operationalisation of concepts is not more or less identical. In this respect the findings are in accordance with the three earlier studies and the interpretations of Walton (1981) and Lammers (1983). However, if the measures of the two approaches <u>do</u> consist of the same items, convergence may arise. In the present study, this was demonstrated in respect of the operationalisations of the concepts: job security, discomfort of working conditions, irregular work schedules and participation in decision-making.

Thus, the results contradict the Walton argument, that no convergence between the two approaches is to be expected, if the levels of analysis differ. In this study the institutional method was directed at the company level and the questionnaire approach to the level of the individual's job. Nevertheless, convergence between the two approaches could be shown for those concepts, which were operationalised in the same way.

The effect of non-response rates and sample sizes

It has already been demonstrated that the non-response rates of the questionnaire measures in the studies of Pennings (1973), Sathe (1978) and Ford (1979) were rather high (or not even mentioned). This circumstance must have been rather disadvantageous for both the representativeness and the size of the samples per organisation. According to the findings in this study, this is an extremely important issue.

As mentioned above, the response rate to the questionnaire approach was high. Nevertheless, the statistical explanatory "power" of the questionnaire measure improved remarkably in those analyses, where only relatively large samples of employees were included (the $N = 21$ analyses; see Tables 3 and 4). In these larger samples individual fluctuations are less important. Also, the convergence between the measurements of the two methods - computed in absolute values - generally improved somewhat in the N = 21 analyses (see Table 2).

This implies that the findings of Pennings, Sathe and Ford may be less valuable than had been previously thought. In this context, reference must be made to Walton (1981). He showed, that the intramethod results of Pennings (1973) and, to some extent, those of Ford (1979) are not consistent with those reported in the original investigations. In contrast, Sathe's findings, having the best response rate, are consistent with those from each original investigation. In conclusion, it can be said that the usefulness of the questionnaire approach strongly depends on the number of employees being interviewed. It is only when these numbers are sufficiently large, that the questionnaire approach may be considered comparable with, or better than the institutional method.

The applicability of the institutional method to quality of working life

This latter conclusion focuses attention on the central research problems under consideration. It was indicated earlier in this paper that the institutional method has been criticised for its non-neutral character. This criticism was also expressed by the representatives of the labour unions, commenting upon the preliminary research design, and may indeed be called the "prima causa" of this paper. Now the research is complete, however, it might be asked whether this criticism is justified.

An examination of the results concerning this institutional approach reveals that it converges with the questionnaire measures, as long as the operationalisation of concepts is more or less identical (see also paragraph 5.1). The institutional approach can compete with the questionnaire approach in explaining variance in organisational phenomena. If the questionnaire approach does not offer sample sizes which are sufficiently large, the institutional method is superior (see also paragraph 5.2).

The first impression is that these two conclusions are not consistent with the "ideology" criticism. However, it appears that they are. Nijhuis (1984), using data from the same study, showed that diverse types of key spokesmen do indeed offer differentiated scores, when interviewed using the same instruments. For example, it was discovered, that representatives of Work's Councils judged the discomfort in labour conditions to be more serious than did Personnel Officers and Chief Executive Officers. Samples of employees saw more problems in this regard than the representatives of management. These findings are consistent with the "ideology" criticism on the institutional mentioned. However, these divergences between interviewees have been shown to be a semi-constant organisational characteristic (Nijhuis, 1984). In other words, if the judgement of the Personnel Officer of the labour conditions in an organisation is known then, to some extent, the judgement of other people (Work's Council, Production Management, samples of employees) in respect of these characteristics within the same organisation is also known.

Therefore, the overall conclusion must be that the institutional method using data derived from interviews with one (or two) key spokesmen may suffice in many instances, even when measuring the quality of working life. Due to its practical advantages and its low costs the institutional method is preferable to the questionnaire approach. However, there are at least two restrictions that have to be made when forming this general conclusion.

i)   This conclusion only applies to comparative analysis aiming at the organisational level. In case studies, however, the data collection cannot be limited to only one or two spokesmen. In this case, the researcher has to deal with diverse negotiating and conflicting groups of participants. In order to understand the dynamics of organisational life the institutional method by no means suffices (e.g. Bacharach and Lawler, 1980).

ii) When the analysis is pitched at the level of the individual's job use of the questionnaire method is unavoidable.

Finally, one concluding remark has to be made. In this paper conclusions were formulated which differ from the results of previous studies. In those earlier studies the measurements were focused on organisation structure, while this study concentrated on quality of working life. Theoretically, the different topics could explain the differences in results between this study and those of Pennings, Sathe and Ford. Therefore it is advisable, to replicate this study once more in the area of organisation structure.

However, there are two pitfalls in those earlier studies that must be avoided:

   i)   It is necessary to compare measurements which are operationalised in an identical manner;

   ii) The non-response rates of the questionnaire measurements must be rather low, probably 25% or less.

In this paper we discovered, that these two "pitfalls" are of major importance in the comparison between the institutional and questionnaire approaches.

References

Bacharach, S B and Lawler, E J: Power and Politics in Organisations. The Social Psychology of Conflict, Coalitions and Bargaining. Jossey-Bass, San Francisco, 1980.

Campbell, D T and Fiske, D W: Convergent and Discriminant Validation by the Mulititrait-multimethod Matrix. Psychological Bulletin, 1959, 56, 81-106.

Chadwick-Jones, J K, Brown, C A and Nicholson, N: Absence from Work: Its Meaning, Measurement, and Control. International Review of Applied Psychology, 1973, 22, 137-154.

Davis, L E and Cherns, A B and Ass.: The Quality of Working Life. Volume One: Problems, Prospects and the State of the Art. The Free Press. New York 1975.

Ford, J D: Institutional versus Questionnaire measures of Organisational Structure, a Re-examination. Academy of Management Journal, 1979, 22, 601-610.

Gardell, B: Compatibility-incompatibility between Organisation and Individual Values. A Swedish Point of View. In. Davis L E, Cherns A B and Ass. The Quality of Working Life. Volume One Problems, Prospects and the State of the Art. The Free Press, New York, 1975, 317-327.

Groot, de A D: Methodologie. Mouton, Den Haag, 1975, (8th. edition).

Khandwalla, P M: The Design of Organisations. Harcourt, Brace, Jovanovich, New York, 1977.

Koot, W T M: Analyse van organisatiestructuren. Samson, Alphen a/d Rijn, 1980.

Lammers, C J and Hickson, D J: Methodological Convergences. In Lammers, C J and Hickson, D J. Organisations alike and unlike. International and Inter-Institutional Studies in the Sociology of Organisations. Routledge and Kegan Paul. London 1979.

Lammers, C J: Organisaties vergelijkenderwijs. Spectrum, Utrecht/Antwerpen, 1983.

Lawler, E E: Measuring the Psychological Quality of Working Life. The Why and How of it. In Davis, L E, Cherns, A B and Ass. The Quality of Working Life. Volume One. Problems, Prospects and the State of the Art. The Free Press, New York, 1975, 123-134.

Muchinsky, P M: Employee Absenteeism. A Review of the Literature. Journal of Vocational Behaviour, 1977, 10, 316-340.

Nichols, T: Ownership, Control and Ideology. Allen George and Unwin, London, 1969.

Nijhuis, F: Beoordelingen van organisatiekenmerken. PHD-dissertation University of Limburg, 1984.

Nijhuis, F and Soeters, J: Werk en ziekte, een onderzoek bij 51 industriële organisaties in Zuid-Limburg. Maastricht, 1982.

Nunnally, J C: Psychometric Theory. McGraw Hill, New York, 1967.

Pennings, J: Measures of Organisational Structure, a Methodological Note. American Journal of Sociology, 1973, 79, 686-704.

Philipsen, H: Afwezigheid wegens Ziekte. Groningen, Wolters-Noordhof, 1969.

Porter, L W and Steers, R M: Organisational, Work, and Personal Factors in Employee Turnover and Absentéeism. Psychological Bulletin, 1973, 80, 151-176.

Pugh, D S, Hickson, D J, Hinings, C R and Turner, C: Dimensions of Organisation Structure. Administrative Science Quarterly, 1968, 13, 65-105.

Pugh, D S and Hickson, D J (eds.) Organisational Structure in its Context, the Aston Programme I. Saxon House, Westmead, 1976.

Quinn, R P and Staines, G L: The 1977 Quality of Employment Survey. Descriptive Statistics with Comparison Data from 1969-70 and 1972-73 Surveys. Institute for Social Research, Ann Arbor, Michigan, 1978.

Sathe, V: Institutional versus Questionnaire Measures of Organisational Structure. Academy of Management Journal, 1978, 21, 227-238.

Schroër, C, Soeters, J, Nijhuis, F, Custers, T, and Philipsen, H: Werk en Ziekte, deel II de Werknermersenquête. Maastricht, 1984.

Seashore, S E: The Michigan Quality of Work programme: Issues in Measurement, Assessment and Outcome Evaluation. In Ven van de, A H and Joyce, W F: Perspectives on organisation design and behaviour. Wiley, New York, 1981.

Smulders, P G W: Bedrifjfskenmerken en ziekteverzuim in de jaren zestig en tachtig, een vergelijkende studie. PhD-dissertation, University of Limburg, 1984.

Steers, R M and Rhodes, S R: Influence on Employee Attendance, A process model. Journal of Applied Psychology, 1978, 63, 391-407.

Steers, R M and Rhodes, S R: Knowledge and Speculation about Absenteeism. In Goodman, P S and Atkin, R S: Absenteeism. Jossey, Bass, San Francisco, 1984.

Ven A H van de, and Ferry, D L: Measuring and assessing organisations. Wiley-Interscience, New York, 1980.

Walton, R E: Criteria for Quality of Working Life. In Davis, L E, Cherns, A B and Ass. The Quality of Working Life. Volume One Problems, Prospects and the State of the Art. The Free Press, New York, 1975, 91-105.

Walton, E J: The Comparison of Measures of Organisation Structure. Academy of Management Review, 1981, 6, 155-160.

Chapter Eight

COMPUTER ATTITUDES AND RESISTANCE TO THE INTRODUCTION
OF NEW TECHNOLOGIES : A PILOT STUDY

E Rosseel and B Geens

Introduction

Contacts with a well-known computer firm (specialising
in office automation) confirmed our conviction that
new technologies, especially in the sector of office
systems, could be implemented more smoothly, if
research into psychosocial factors were given more
attention. For that reason, the worries and anxieties
which accompany the introduction of computers and
robots in service and production organisations,
deserve particular attention from social scientists.

As the computer, symbolising a New Age of
technological innovation and for some authors even a
third industrial revolution or a Third Wave (Toffler,
1980), penetrates the daily life of more and more
people, attitudes towards the computer diversify.
This whole field of attitudes towards this cultural
object, however, seems scientifically unexplored. As
will be shown in this Chapter, no established concepts
have yet been designed to describe specific computer
attitudes. A rough discrimination exists between
"computer freaks" who show an excessive computer
enthusiasm and people who for several reasons exhibit
manifest forms of computer "anxieties". But how are
these different attitudes to be ordered and
categorised?

Computer attitudes can be studied in two basic ways,
which, in earlier work (Rosseel, 1982), were labelled
System Psychology and Actor Psychology. A system
psychological approach treats the (human) individual
as a medium in a system of external elements. The
psychologist analyses the individual from a supra-

individual viewpoint which is the system under consideration, for example an organisation. The vocabulary of the analysis refers to system-desired states; it does not refer to the action perspective of the person. Our classic example of a system psychological term is "absenteeism" : the word does not say anything about the absent person himself but about the system that is troubled by his absence. In that way, system psychology regularly makes use of negative descriptive terms, e.g. "X is low on Machiavellianism". In general, system psychology is integrated in a social practice of behaviour control aimed at optimalisation of the functioning of social systems. System psychology grasps all individuals by the same language. In samples, individuals are averaged, the person's specificity is abolished.

As many institutions of society are primarily interested in the optimal functioning of systems (composed of human individuals among other components), psychologists who identify themselves with these institutional interests, tend to a system psychological approach, as this approach seems more economically justified. System psychology, in practice, aims at a general strategy that makes abstractions of the idiosyncracies of the particular cases : the probablistic error that is induced, is considered to be less serious than the costs of an every time repeated case-study.

No guarantee exists that this approach is really superior : system psychologists try to solve a management problem by psychological reductionism as the complexity of the problem has been sacrificed for uniformity. A psychological analysis that leaves the personal specificity and the complexity of the particular case intact will, from a practical viewpoint, in each case give complementary enriching insights.

Actor pyschology tries to understand the person from within, as an autopoetic system (Maturana and Varela, 1980), i.e. an autonomous self-organised system that cannot be explained by reference to an environmental output or an external observer. As a human person functions as the observer of his own actions, actor psychology can unfold the logic of a person's behaviour by analysing the way a person monitors and justifies his actions (De Waele and Harre, 1976).

145

So, two lines of research are open to the researcher. Actor psychology concentrates upon the person-specific aspects of computer attitudes and their integration in the action perspective of the person. Within this perspective research programmes tackle the following questions :

a) which are the verbal statements and the overt acts by which the person gives expression to his relation with the phenomenon "computer" (in so far as the "computer" belongs to his "life space")?

b) how are these manifestations organised on the personal level?

c) how are they integrated in other cognitive structures and acts of the person?

d) which action perspective expresses <u>personal meaning</u>? (e.g. what does it mean to become a professional systems analyst?)

Industrial and organisational psychologists, however, will most probably study computer attitudes within a system psychological approach, as industrial and organisational psychology has established as its goal not the knowledge of persons but a contribution to the effective control of the work organisation. Most industrial and organisational psychologists will define their role as "change agents" who try to optimise the implementation of new technologies (e.g. De Corte and Coetsier, 1983). The system wherein computer attitudes are integrated, can be represented as :

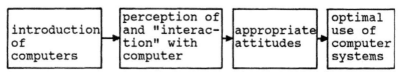

Of course, the model which represents the optimal state of the envisaged system, is too general; all "boxes" are vague and remain meaningless if no refinements are specified with regard to three points

a) who are the individuals who are being confronted with the "introduction of the computer?"

b) who is the "observer" who considers the system from the outside and has an interest in its optimal state?

c) what type of "computer system" is meant precisely?

The situation most commonly thought of concerns a management ("the observer") that reorganises a production department of an office by the introduction of automated systems. The "computer system" is a more or less centralised network of hardware apparatus and the "individuals" are the personnel (or what remains of them) who have to adapt technically and attitudinally to the new equipment. However, another interesting situation is posed by a salesman of a computer firm ("the observer") who tries to convince an individual manager (the "individual") to substitute a personal computer for some or all of the functions of his secretary. "Introduction" here does not mean much more than visual presentation. A second deficiency of the model concerns the too simplistic time dimension suggested by the model : people have ideas, attitudes and expectations about computers and working with computers before they have "physical contact" with them.

A more complicated, and still simplistic version of the model could therefore be represented as:

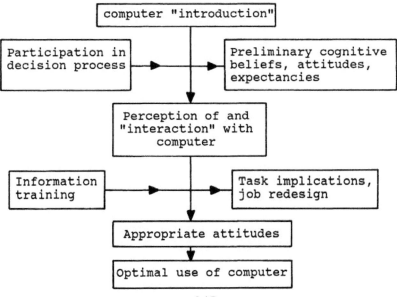

The most serious problem faced by computer firms and by management in general, concerns resistance to the introduction of computers, mostly due to worries about loss of job stability and job security. So most efforts will be directed to the understanding of "computer resistance". Generally speaking, two aberrations may threaten the homeostasis of the system:

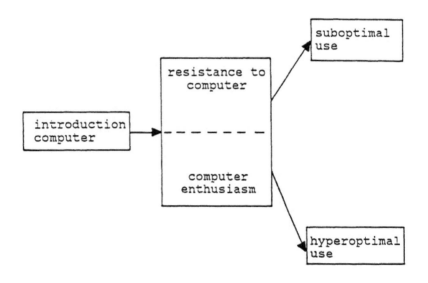

In a system psychological perspective, the task confronted by the researcher is to design a set of descriptive terms (related to computer-attitudes) that can be applied to all individuals. Roughly speaking, this means an investigation of three elements :

a) <u>cognitive elements</u>: what does the individual know about computers?

b) <u>affective elements</u>: what emotions are elicited by the phenomenon computer?

c) <u>cognitive elements</u>: how do people relate to computers?

Organisational surveys of computer attitudes may be very useful at the moment of the introduction of automated technology to the office or the shopfloor. This seems so evident that one is astonished by the scarcity of the available literature concerning computer attitudes. In each case, no established set of concepts exists at the present moment. Shye and Elizur (1976) speak about deprivation of job rewards, and they distinguish worries with reference to four domains : job security, job stability, job proficiency, and job interest. Using partial order scalogram analysis they succeed in ordering these worries according to their intensity (the number of worries a person holds) and to their content (job intrinsic vs. job extrinsic). Unfortunately, their study looks more like an exercise in partial order scalogram analysis than like an exploration of computer attitudes. A number of studies concern attitudes of children who are faced with some form of computer aided education (Reece and Gable, 1982; Lawton and Gerschner, 1982). Zoltan and Chapanis (1982), in a study of computer attitudes among professionals, distinguish between three attitudinal clusters : "computers as efficient machines", "depersonalising characteristics" and "user's enthusiasm".

However, as far as we can overview the situation, the pertinent attitudes of employees are seldom taken into account when office automation is implemented. The psychosocial resistances to the introduction of computers at the office, are most of the time interpreted in terms of the classical "resistance to change" (Sanders and Birkin, 1980; De Corte and Coetsier, 1983), with the consequence that no appropriate analysis of computer attitudes is undertaken.

Nevertheless, a general consensus exists that negative attitudes towards computers result in distrustful reception of office computers, a difficult integration of the computer in the work flow and a lengthening of the implementation times of automated systems. The strategy used to cope with these resistances remains the classic solution of Coch and French's original study about "resistance to change" (Coch and French, 1948) : participation in the decision process (Koopman, 1981).

The social and ideological impact of the computer is, in our opinion, a strong argument for a particular analysis of computer attitudes and "computer anxieties". This report forms a part of larger projects which aim to explore computer attitudes and to link them to the behaviour of individual people and groups. On the one hand, computer attitudes will be studied actor-psychologically by referring to the person's action perspective; on the other hand, computer attitudes will be analysed system psychologically by the construction of a set of general concepts that can be linked to other organisational variables.

The study described here is a first attempt to explore the cognitive and affective dimensions of computer attitudes among clerical personnel who have never before worked with computers but who in the near future will be confronted with office automation. The aim of the study was twofold :

1. To explore the dimensions of computer attitudes by the analysis of a first version of an inventory of statements reflecting computer attitudes. This was expected to result in an inventory of computer attitudes.

2. To generate hypotheses concerning the relationships between computer attitudes and personal variables such as sex, age, occupational level and type of firms (especially private enterprises versus public agencies). Special attention was to be paid to the relationships between perceived job characteristics (autonomy, responsibility, perceived promotion opportunities etc.) and computer attitudes.

Method

As no research instruments relevant to computer attitudes were available, a first version of an instrument that could be used as an inventory of computer attitudes in organisational surveys, was designed in two phases. In a first phase, some 20 employed persons, mostly clericals, were interviewed about their attitudes to computers and the introduction of computers at the office, in order to produce a set of statements that could be treated as items of a questionnaire. This phase resulted in a set of 58 statements which could be regrouped under 11 topics :

1. Diagnostic of the actual job (7 statements)

   e.g. Management generally puts our suggestions into practice.

2. **"Knowledge" and cognitive beliefs about computers**
    (9 statements)

    e.g. The computer can think autonomously.

3. **Acceptance of re-training** (3 statements)

    e.g. I should feel humiliated if I had to follow
    courses about computers.

4. **Fear of computers** (5 statements)

    e.g. I will only work with computers if I am
    forced to.

5. **Experience of work - after introduction of
    computers** (9 statements)

    e.g. Working with computers is dull and
    monotonous.

6. **Stress** (4 statements)

    e.g. Working with computers will ask a lot more
    of my concentration for months.

7. **Impact upon social contacts** (6 statements)

    e.g. The computer will foster the cooperation
    between my department and others of the firm.

8. **Impact upon status and promotion** (7 statements)

    e.g. As a status symbol, the computer will give
    me a new feeling of status.

9. **Modalities of implementation** (3 statements)

    e.g. I liked the fact that the introduction of
    the computer would be discussed with the
    personnel.

10. **Confidence in computers** (3 statements)

    e.g I will not store up documents that the
    computer has made superfluous.

11. <u>Privacy</u> (2 statements)

> e.g. I would not mind personal data being stored in the computer even if they are accessible to others.

This list of 58 statements was administered to a small sample of 10 students and employees to test the readability and unambiguousness of the items. As a result, some items were adapted. Items were to be rated on agreement by means of a five point scale.

To get insight in the underlying dimensions of computer attitudes and to generate hypotheses about relationships with personal variables, a set of 20 questionnaires were brought to 20 administrative organisations located in and around Brussels : the personnel manager was asked to distribute the questionnaires among those clerical workers in the company who had never worked upon computers. After two weeks, a second contact was made to pick up the completed questionnaires.

A total of 103 questionnaires could be retained for further analysis. It is understood, of course, that this sample is in no way representative of the population of clerical workers and the response profiles cannot give any idea about how all clerical workers think about computers : the results are indicative and must be seen in the light of the composition of the sample.

<u>The composition of the sample.</u>

Due to a fault in the reproduction of the questionnaire, the question about the sex of the respondent was missing in the sets sent to some firms. So, only 66% of the cases mention their sex. A great majority of the sample (52 out of 103) however were male.

Ages ranged from 19 to 62 : the mean age was 35 years. Tenure ranged from 1 (and less) to 35 years : mean tenure was 10 years. Occupational level was well diversified : 11% being lower-skilled, 47% qualified clerical workers, 25% bottom and middle managers, 9% staff personnel and 5% higher executives. Educational level reflected this occupational composition : more than half of the sample had completed high school, college or university education. Fourteen organisations participated in the study. Roughly speaking, half of the respondents were public servants, the other half worked in private corporations.

Of course, these personal variables were not independent of each other. Sex was significantly associated with age (ordinal gamma =-0.48), males being older; with educational level (gamma =-0.50), males being of higher educational level; and with occupational level (gamma =-.68), males occupying higher job positions. Age was evidently associated with tenure (Pearson's r = .69z, p<.001) and with type of firm (chi-square = 10.7; df = 2; p<.01) : the age categories less than 30 and 41+ were over represented in the private corporations; the age category 31-40 in the public agencies. Tenure was associated with educational level : staff personnel and top managers have lower tenure (chi-square = 8.3; df = 3; p<.04). Educational level had evidently a strong association with occupational level (chi-square = 21.8; df = 9; p<.01). Occupational level was associated with type of firm (chi-square = 8.1; df = 3; p<.05) : respondents from the public sector have higher job positions.

Results

1. The structure of computer attitudes.

The underlying structure of the 58 statements was revealed by Smallest Space Analysis (Lingoes, 1973), a technique for representing the similarities between "objects" into a spatial configuration. Given a matrix of intercorrelations, a two-dimensional configuration of the 58 statements was produced with a coefficient of alienation of .27; this configuration was confirmed in a three-dimensional solution with a coefficient of alienation of .21. The third dimension however was not confirmed in a four-dimensional solution. Figure 1 reproduces the two-dimensional configuration.

153

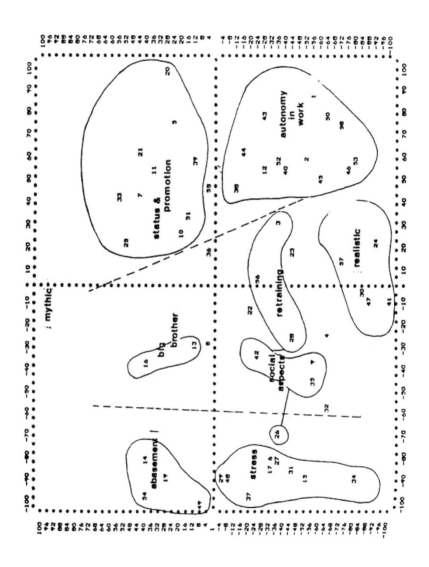

Figure 1 : SSA-configuration of 58 statements.

The oppositions of this structure are very clear. The left - right dimension opposes job and career involvement which is linked to positive computer attitudes, whereas non-involvement is linked to negative computer attitudes. The top-bottom dimension opposes a realistic view of the computer to a more unrealistic and emotionally loaded view.

The regional structure can roughly be divided into three parts. The <u>left region</u> contains the statements that deny the positive value of the computer. The "abasement" cluster sees working on the computer as a humiliation (54) and resistance to following courses is expressed (14). The computer is experienced as threatening. The <u>stress cluster</u> synthesises some anticipated negative effects of computers: less social contacts (29); closer supervision of the work to be done (48); nervousness (6,17); dull and monotonous task content (27). There is no spontaneous tendency to work with computers (15,31). Knowledge about computers is superficial and limited to mass media information (item 34). This rejection of the computer seems to be associated with low-skilled jobs with few intrinsic job qualities.

The right region groups the statements that express positive computer attitudes. In the upper right region are attitudes of people who are <u>preoccupied with promotion</u> and who see the computer as a means towards promotion (33, 39, 51). The computer is uncritically accepted and the enthusiasm is unlimited: no objection against invasion of privacy (11); 100% confidence in computer output (10,21); no need for preparatory courses or retraining is felt (25). The <u>"autonomy in work" cluster</u> contains the items that diagnose the actual job as interesting and giving opportunity for autonomous action and use of skills and abilities (1, 12, 40, 45, 46, 50). People in these jobs see the computer as an aid for better job performance (43, 50); they believe that the implementation of office automation will provide them with a wider range of social contacts in the organisation (38, 43, 44) and they say they have a clear picture of what a computer really is (2).

The middle region encompasses cognitive beliefs about the computer. The emotional loaded clusters "abasement" and "status" share come mythical ideas about computers (13 = the computer can think autonomously !). A more realistic and factual view about computers as an efficient man-monitored automate

(24, 41, 47, 57) and an awareness of the need for retraining are especially typical of the "autonomy-in-work" people. Consideration of social aspects (fear of unemployment, 26, 35, 42,) is associated with the "stress" cluster.

This cognitive structure gives a neatly arranged picture of computer attitudes. The two dimensions acceptance-rejection and realistic-mythic appear as the basic dimensions along which computer attitudes can be ordered. It should be emphasised that this solution clearly indicates that mythical ideas about computers are not the exclusive property of people who fear the introduction of computers. Those who wait impatiently for the computer's introduction in order to realise their desires for promotion, are equally predisposed to develop a deformed and unrealistic image of the computer.

Of course, this structure is constrained by its input. If the 58 items do not cover the whole "universe" of computer attitudes, the configurational solution may be of little general value. Further research will have to test the generality of the structure.

Can the "clusters" be treated as psychometric scales ? The internal consistency, as measured by Cronbach's alpha sets no problem for the clusters "autonomy" (alpha = .82), "stress" (alpha = .77) and "status" (alpha = .67). Problematic are "realistic" (alpha = .57; if item 30 is deleted, alpha = .60). "abasement" (alpha = .64) and "social aspects" (alpha = .54; if item 9 is deleted, alpha = .57). Plainly bad are the clusters: "retraining" (alpha = .38; if item 56 is deleted, alpha = .49) and "big brother" (alpha = .15), which have respectively only three and two items. Internal consistency of the problematic clusters could substantially be raised if supplementary items would be formulated (especially for the small clusters "retraining", "social aspects" and "big brother").

2. Hypotheses concerning relationships with personal variables

As our sample is in no way representative of the population of clerical workers, the following results are purely indicative and must be confirmed by further analysis. In the same way, the frequency distributions of the responses on the attitudinal statements have no general value. Nevertheless, it is interesting to see what items receive high agreement and what are negatively endorsed.

Table 1: Positively Endorsed Items

(rating range 1-5 : agreement - non agreement)

		Mean
(41)	The computer is an automate that only executes what people impose upon it	1.53
(24)	The computer can only process the instructions that we have given it	1.58
(58)	The computer is an aid that enables me to perform better	1.76
(2)	I have in my mind an image of what a computer looks like	1.81
(9)	I wish that the introduction of computers would be discussed with the personnel	1.81
(55)	The computer works faster and more accurately than man	1.91
(57)	The computer will take over a lot of human tasks	1.93

Most of these positively endorsed items belong to the cluster of "realistic view of the computer". This can be due to the rather high educational level of the sample.

Table 2: Negatively Endorsed Items

	Mean
(14) I should feel humiliated if I was obliged to attend computer courses	4.38
(54) I experience working with computers as a form of humiliation	4.38
(13) The computer can think autonomously	4.10
(11) I would <u>not</u> mind personal data being stored in the computer even if they are accessible to others	4.08
(25) I think that I could work upon computers without preparatory courses	4.04
(49) The computer limits me	4.01

These negatively endorsed items concern the emotional rejection of computers (the "abasement"-cluster). Infraction upon privacy is also rejected. Further on, mythic ideas are not very widespread in our sample.

2.1 Relationships with sex.

Relationships between computer attitudes and personal variables were analysed using chi-square tests, ordinal gamma and Pearson's product-moment correlation coefficient measures. For sex, relationships are tabled as significant if gamma exceeds .40 and Pearson's meets the significance level of $p<.05$. However, we must keep in mind that only 14 females are compared with 52 males.

Table 3: Computer attitudes and sex

	g	r
(39) The introduction of the computer will raise my status and power	.74	.42
(58) The computer is an aid for performing better	.70	.41
(25) I think I could work with computers without preparatory courses	.70	.28
(52) My actual job is very important	.67	.42
(53) The computer also creates new jobs	.59	.40
(5) My work will be more meaningful after automation	.59	.35
(45) My actual job offers me status based on knowledge and experience	.57	.34
(37) I can't concentrate on my job	-.56	-.35
(26) The computer will cause new unemployment	- .56	-.32
(6) Work will be more hurried after the introduction of computers	-.45	-.25
(44) After the introduction of computers, I will have more contacts with my supervisors	.44	.24
(13) The computer can think autonomously	-.42	-.24
(18) Cooperation between departments will be better after automation	.41	.23
(34) My knowledge of computers is limited to mass media information	-.41	-.21
(48) I will be troubled if the computer will control my efficiency	-.40	-.23

159

Positive signs are "masculine" items; negative are "feminine" items. The general picture of Table 3 lets us conclude that males are in better positions and see more positive effects of computers whereas females who occupy less interesting jobs, are more worried about unemployment and fear an increase in job stress.

However, as we have seen, sex is associated with educational and occupational level and in that way no conclusion can be made with regard to attitudes based on sex itself. Another word of caution is necessary : "masculinity" of an item does not mean that all males endorse the items : e.g. "increase in status and power" is anticipated by "only" 17% of males but by no females; 42% females think computers can act autonomously, against 18% of the males.

2.2 Relationships with Age.

Age was divided into three categories : less than 30, 31-40 and 40+. Associations were analysed using ordinal gamma; gammas exceeding .25 are listed in Table 4. Positive gamma's indicate higher agreement by young people.

Table 4 Relationships with age

		g
(58)	The computer is an aid for performing better	-.50
(46)	My actual job is based upon knowledge, experience and use of my abilities	-.50
(45)	My actual job offers me status based upon knowledge and experience	-.46
(24)	The computer can only process our instructions	-.37
(30)	After the introduction of the computer I will try to maintain my status and position	-.33
(41)	The computer is an automate that only executes what people impose upon it	-.32
(13)	The computer can think autonomously	.32
(34)	My knowledge about computers is limited to mass media information	-.25
(33)	I have real opportunities for advancement	.25

Summarising Table 4, we can conclude that the older people of our sample occupy intrinsically satisfying jobs and have a "realistic" view of computers. Mythical ideas about computers (item 13) are more typical for younger employees. This at first sight is a surprising result, which can only partially be explained by the association between age and sex. A better explanation can be provided by referring to difference in the "career phase" : older people have reached career stability, feel less threatened by the computer and can thus develop a less emotional attitude against computers. Younger people must still make themselves a career (which explains the association with item 33), the career stress can tempt them to more imaginative views of computers.

2.3 <u>Relationship with educational level.</u>

Four educational levels were taken into account : lower secondary, higher secondary, higher non-university, university.

As educational level can be treated as an ordinal variable but not as an interval variable, only ordinal gamma was taken into consideration. Gamma's above .25 (Tables are 5 x 4 instead of 5 x 2 in the case of sex) are listed in Table 5. Positive gamma's indicate that lower levels agree more with the statement.

<u>Table 5 Relationships with Educational Level</u>

	g
(13) The computer can think autonomously	.38
(26) The computer will cause new unemployment	.37
(58) The computer is an aid for performing better	-.34
(5) My job will be more meaningful after automation	-.27
(48) I will be troubled if the computer will control my efficiency	.26
(6) Work will be more hurried after the introduction of computers	.25
(17) Working with the computer makes me nervous	.25

Only seven statements reach high gamma values. Most items are also listed in the table of relationships with sex. The items which express the better job position of males show the values falling off. This implies that the occupation of intrinsically satisfying jobs seems to be bound more to sex than to educational level, a result that will please the feminists. The worries women have about computers, can thus be due to their low occupational status. The general conclusion for educational level is simple : low levels fear more repercussions upon job stress and worry about mythical aspects of the computer.

2.4 Relationships with Occupational Level.

Four occupational levels were considered : low-level administrative jobs, qualified clerical jobs, lower management, staff functions and higher management. Positive gamma's in Table 6 indicate that lower levels agree more with the statement.

Table 6   Relationships with Occupational Level

		g
(13)	The computer can think autonomously	.47
(6)	Work will be more hurried after the introduction of the computer	.36
(17)	Working with the computer will make me nervous	.34
(28)	Working with computers will ask a lot more of my concentration for months	.33
(53)	The computer also creates new jobs	-.33
(27)	Working with computers is dull and monotonous	.31
(35)	Office automation will cost a lot of jobs	.30
(48)	I will be troubled if the computer controls my efficiency	.30
(24)	The computer can only process our instructions	-.30
(44)	After the introduction of computers, I will have more contacts with my supervisors	.30
(43)	The computer will help me to be creative	-.27

The general picture looks the same as in the case of sex and educational level. However, as for educational level, no associations are found with actual job characteristics, a rather bizarre result. Low occupational levels manifest an anticipation of increased job stress and fear of unemployment. Managers and staff personnel hold more positive attitudes and are more ready to integrate the computer in their daily tasks.

2.5 <u>Relationships with type of firm.</u>

In this section, a comparison is made between personnel working in public agencies and personnel in private corporations. Ordinal gamma's above .40 and Pearson's meeting the p< .05 level are considered.

<u>Table 7   Relationships with type of firm</u>

		g	r
(58)	The computer is an aid for performing better	.56	.31
(12)	In my actual job I gain experience that can serve my career	.52	.36
(1)	In my actual job I get the opportunity to use my abilities	.50	.38
(54)	I experience working with the computer as a form of humiliation	-.46	-.20
(52)	My job is important for the firm	.45	.30
(2)	I have an image of what a computer looks like	.42	.25

Most significant associations concern differences in the experience of work : public employees experience their work as less intrinsically meaningful. Nevertheless, there are indications that public servants have more negative attitudes towards computers even if their occupational level is not lower. These results reflect the general "malaise" which prevails in the public sector due to over-bureaucratisation, and the absence of real personnel management. (Van Raemdonck, 1983).

Conclusions

In two ways, the results of this pilot study are promising. The revealed structure of computer attitudes offers an interesting categorisation which, after having been confirmed in replication studies of more representative samples, could form the basis for an Inventory of Computer Attitudes. However, an attempt should be made to fill up the more empty regions of the SSA mapping.

On the other hand, interesting hypotheses concerning the relationships between computer attitudes and personal variables were generated. They also, must be confirmed by subsequent research. Most interesting is the question of whether women, independently of their occupational status, are really less computer-minded. If so, this would confirm the more anecdotal observation from classroom experience and the participation at computer holiday courses, which seems to indicate that schoolgirls find computers less attractive. This attitudinal trend could have an important impact upon women's position within the labour market.

The practical implications of knowledge about computer attitudes are evident. Organisational surveys before and during the implementation of office automation can be useful for the way personnel should be informed, for better modalities of implementation, for determining the kinds of technical and attitudinal training needed and for detecting the groups of personnel that may pose particular problems.

A first step for overcoming resistance to change in any case might be to provide the means for detecting the group of computer "supporters" and of the group of computer "opponents". The present research instrument, especially if it could be psychometrically refined, can fulfill this role and is even able to describe the basis of negative attitudes to computers. More intensive techniques could then deepen the insight into the specific and negative attitudes wherein resistance against computers are rooted.

If negative attitudes to computers are deep-rooted and strongly integrated in more encompassing belief and attitude systems, strategies for changing attitudes will possibly fall beyond the control of individual organisations.

References

Coch, L and French J R P (1948): Overcoming resistance
to change, Human Relations, 11, 512-532

De Corte, W and Coetsier, P (1983): De invoering van
nieuwe technologieen. (The introduction of new
technologies) Economisch en Sociaal Tijdschrift
37, 145-160.

De Waele, J P and Harre, R (1976): The Personality of
Individuals. In : Harre, R: Personality, Oxford,
Blackwell.

Koopman, P L (1981): Towards a contingency approach
for users' participation in automation.
Amsterdam, Vrije Universiteit.

Lawton, J and Gerschner, V T (1982): A review of the
literature on attitudes toward computers and
computerized instruction. Journal of Research and
Development in Education, 16, 50-55.

Lingoes, J C (1973): The Guttman-Lingoes Nonmetric
Program Series. Ann Arbor, Mathematics Press.

Maturana, H R and Varela, F J (1980): Autopoeisis and
cognition. Dordrecht, Reidel.

Reece, M J and Gable, R K (1982): The development and
validation of a measure of general attitudes
toward computers. Educational and Psychological
Measurement, 42, 913-916.

Rosseel, E (1982): Arbeidsorientaties : conceptual
analyse en empirisch onderzoek. (Orientations to
work : conceptual analysis and an empirical
study). Unpublished doctoral dissertation.
Brussels, Vrije Universiteit Brussel.

Sanders, D and Birkin, J (1980): Computer and
Management in a changing Society. New York, Mc
Graw-Hill.

Shye, S and Elizur, D: (1976) Worries about
Deprivation of job rewards following
Computerization. Human Relations, 29, 63-71.

Toffler, A (1980): The Third Wave. New York, Random
House.

INTRODUCTION OF NEW TECHNOLOGIES

Van Raemdonck, E et al. (1983):   Automation in public
    agencies. Leuven, Acco.

Zoltan, E and Chapanis, A (1982):   What do
    professional persons think about computers?
    Behaviour and Information Technology, 1, 55-68.

Chapter Nine

METHODOLOGICAL ISSUES IN THE ASSESSMENT OF MANAGEMENT
DEVELOPMENT

D Ashton

Introduction

The reflections in this paper have arisen directly
from a practical problem within a major multinational
organisation. Until July 1986, the author was a
senior manager in BAT Industries, responsible for
management development programmes on an international
basis. This paper is based on that experience. This
has centred on the means by which information might be
gathered to clarify and support various strategic
decisions on manager education and development within
the company. Specifically, two kinds of strategic
issues were of concern - firstly, the actual effects
of general management programmes on senior managers
and, secondly, the changing future needs for general
manager performance in our different businesses and
the likely effects these changes would have on
requirements for manager education. In order to
determine the appropriate approach to data collection,
it was necessary to step back and, as is shown in this
paper, to reflect upon the basic choice which needed
to be made. This choice was either to look towards an
established survey approach as one solution or a more
informal and less structured qualitative approach
which would involve immersion in managers' working
experience and problems. The balance of this paper
therefore will address the particular features and
benefits of one survey approach and, in conclusion,
make some comparison with the alternative qualitative
approach.

Since I continue to see management education as a subsystem of overall management development in the
organisation, it may be that my information needs have
not changed so much from 14 years, ago when I began
working with large, regionally-based organisations
while at Durham University Business School. I led a
unit which developed the Management Development Audit
- a survey questionnaire approach which was
subsequently applied across 20 different industries.

The bulk of this paper therefore is concerned
initially to look at the Management Development Audit
and then to make some comparison of that with an
alternative approach. The paper will therefore be
concerned primarily with how data might be collected
in this area - not on what those data should be.

Survey Intervention

Before dealing with the specific intentions of the
Management Development Audit, it may be useful
briefly to discuss the purposes and problems
associated with organisational interventions of this
kind. Argyris (1970) has reminded us that the aim of
any intervention should be to improve the
effectiveness of the organisation. In the case of an
organisational survey, a specific objective will be to
obtain accurate information. Related to this
objective are two implicit conditions for the
effectiveness of the intervention; firstly, that in
generating the data there will be a climate for free
choice about the consequent action which should be
taken; secondly, that there will be a commitment to
making that action or change actually work. Clearly
this view makes sense - there is little point in
generating data if it is not to be used in some
positive way to improve effectiveness. However, some
people have pointed to the potential problem of the
"politics" of information. Any intervention -
particularly one in which questionnaires are issued as
part of surveys on a wide scale - should be aware of
the political nature of information and have planned,
in advance, the ways in which the effective use of
that data will be used and probable effectiveness
improved.

As an organisational intervention, the Management
Development Audit has three specific features which
help to achieve its intended effects:

1. It identifies a client for the survey - often data
    collection of this kind runs into trouble where
    client identification is not clearly achieved. In
    this case the client or clients must be a member
    or members of top management, in order to accept
    responsibility for the overall results.

2. The survey approach is able to generate data at
    different levels. This helps to make comparison
    between the response of one department and another

and between a variety of different groupings of
the employee and management population.

3. The third attraction of this survey approach is
    the apparent objectivity of the data when
    generated and analysed. This arises not only
    because the data has been seen to be collected in
    a standard way from a large sample or a total
    management population, but also because the
    analysis of the data presents statistically sound
    data in a numerical form which reinforces its
    validity.

Where this approach has worked best there is clear
commitment to other important and positive features.
These include commitment to the outcomes of the
analysis and the major conclusions to which the survey
points. These conclusions are normally presented in a
form which indicates clearly the lines for desired
change and top management decision-making. Because
the data are collected from large numbers of employees
within the company, there is also an implicit
commitment to communicate the findings and most often
also the agreed changes for improvements.

Necessary pre-conditions for success, however for this
survey approach are a climate in which there is a
positive view about the survey itself and a
commitment, if necessary, for change following the
findings of the survey. There must also be a climate
in which the participation of management in generating
data for top management decision-making is accepted.

Development of the Management Development Audit

This survey approach was developed in three
distinctive stages:

1. A persistent, relatively general enquiry had been
    arising in discussions with larger client
    companies with whom I and my colleagues were
    working on the development of management
    development programmes. This enquiry revolved not
    around the content of the activities companies
    were undertaking in management development, but
    how effective their efforts actually were.

    Answers to such general questions most often took
    the form of subjective opinions which, when
    examined or tested, provided evidence which was

very limited and primarily anecdotal - for example:

> "why, only the other day someone told me that their manager was very poor at running an appraisal session."

To make proposals for further action in management development required a more detailed objective understanding of the present state of "health" of management development in the organisation. It also appeared to be true that, the more senior the manager, the less their grasp of the reality of management development in their own organisation. Around this general and ill-defined question a research approach began to evolve.

2. The second stage involved the classic research problem - that is:

> "Try to find out what we need to find out".

This was done through a series of extensive semi-structured interviews with managers in three organisations. The theme of these discussions was their experience and views of management development. These data were carefully compared and analysed - and certain patterns did begin to emerge. In particular, from these early studies - and it was confirmed by other studies later - we were able to lay out a framework for the analysis of management development. This framework identified the major components of management development and their relationships in the organisation.

This framework can perhaps be most clearly demonstrated by a system model analysing management development which is laid out in Figure 1.

Figure 1 indicates three core sub-systems in management development - appraisal, career development and development activities.

Figure 1   A framework for analysis of management
                          development

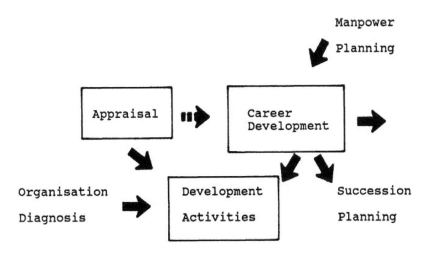

Elements: activity level, involvement, information
- up and down, planning, assessment

The connecting arrows show the movement of
information and the relationships between these
three internal sub-systems. Appraisal can
therefore be seen primarily as an information
generating system, career development as a
decision-making system and development activities
as an activity-based system.

It is possible to examine individually each of
these three sub-systems - and to assess the
relative levels of involvement of managers, the
way in which information is passed up or down, the
extent to which activities within the system are
planned and the extent to which there is any kind
of built-in assessment of the activity.

But these three sub-systems of management development do not stand alone. In reality, management development ties into other areas of personnel/human resources policies. It also is linked to organisational performance and the achievement of organisational goals. The other immediate sub-systems of personnel/human resources within an organisation which seem to relate directly to management development are identified as manpower planning and succession planning. Both have a strong link to the decisions in career development. Additionally, organisation diagnosis - the identification of requirements for change in the organisation - has a strong impact upon the content of certain development activities.

It is important to note that this framework of analysis emerged _after_ this second exploratory stage in organisations and was not developed as a hypothesis for testing before the investigation was undertaken.

3. Out of the loose, but very illuminating process of extensive interviews with managers in three companies came the opportunity to develop the third and final stage. This identified specific questions which would cover the range of issues likely to be faced in any organisation about management development, and whose answers could also be easily coded. The development and testing of this third stage enabled the number of key questions in all three key areas of management development to be significantly reduced, thus making the survey approach more manageable. Further, it became clear that using the survey questions it would be possible to draw comparisons between three sets of perceptions:

a) Management development as it is supposed to be,

b) Management development as managers experience it, and

c) Management development as managers would like it to be.

The sources of the first of these sets of general perceptions, i.e. the formal picture, was acquired by interviewing top management and examining formal policy documents within the organisation. Data for the second and third sets of perceptions were collected primarily through the questionnaires issued to managers at different levels within the organisation.

In this relatively simple way of comparing these three sets of perceptions - supported directly by data derived from analysis of the questionnaires - we were able to identify very clearly major inconsistencies, issues and points of concern as well as achievements in an organisation's management development systems.

The Audit Process

The development of the management audit produced a specific process for conducting it. Details of the process and case studies of its application have been published elsewhere (Easterby-Smith, Braiden, and Ashton 1980) but the broad steps in this were as follows:

1. Using a standard checklist to identify "the formal picture", i.e. management development "as it is supposed to be", drawn from policy and procedure documents together with interviews with top management.

2. A pilot package of questionnaires was then put together. Within the questionnaires there was some choice - between formal and informal versions of the appraisal system and career development system. (A formal system meant one which had a declared policy, which had been communicated to some or all of the management. An informal system reflected the reality that information was generated and actions took place, without there being associated formal procedures or policy).

3. The questionnaires, including more general questions on the company environment and general attitudes to management development, would be issued to a pilot group. The main objectives of the pilot were to check for any problems of understanding the standard questions and to develop a tailor-made glossary of interpretation of terms - such as "senior" or "middle" management - using definitions with gradings appropriate to the particular organisation being surveyed.

4. Once the pilot had been run and the appropriate glossary produced, there were final decisions about additional questions which management were

particularly interested in answering with the survey and these would be also built into the questionnaires.

5. Consideration was also given in these early stages to the means by which the audit should be introduced. Sometimes this would be through group meetings with different levels of management, sometimes through a letter from the chief executive to all managers.

6. Questionnaires were then issued, with an understanding that the answers would be treated confidentially and analysed externally by the University team.

7. Data was analysed through a computer and the results were then available for interpretation and discussion before being fed-back.

Associated Roles

It is important at this stage to explain the variety of roles associated with the audit process. The University team were the outside consultants, which worked with two key groups inside the company. Firstly, nominated specialists usually from the personnel function, whose responsibility it would be to stay with the audit at each stage - they were particularly associated with the detailed analysis of the results. The second group were the identified group of "clients" within the company who would formally accept the project work and its results. This latter group was particularly important in the final stage when results were fed-back and decisions taken about consequent actions.

Thus, it was always clear that the ownership of the output rested firmly with the clients and their staff and not with the audit team.

(Across the 20 or so industries in which the audit approach was applied, it was interesting to notice how varied were the specific issues in management development for a particular company and the subsequent strategic changes were also markedly different from one organisation to another.)

Key Strengths and Limitations

In retrospect, one key strength of the management development audit approach revolved around its credibility in generating useful information where there had previously been little or only poor data. In practice, it was possible to hold convincing and positive discussions with top management about the health of their management development systems, and help them focus on decisions which they should take about required changes.

The limitations might be expected to outnumber the strengths - but not necessarily to outweigh them. For example, in taking a system view, identifying the three main sub-systems as appraisal, career development and training/development activities, a strong emphasis is put upon a _particular_ view of management development in the organisation. It is _not_ that this view has subsequently turned out to be invalid - it still seems to make a lot of sense as a way of explaining management development. However, there are other ways of looking at management development!

This approach tends to highlight issues around each of the major sub-systems as described above, but it does not necessarily encourage more detailed understanding of particular parts of the system. Further, it is only a static "snapshot", like a balance sheet, at one point in time. Other limitations would include the kind of data which the audit approach generates. It is essentially survey-based - asking managers to respond by allocating their answers into particular "boxes". The strength's approach mainly resides in the numerical analysis of the managers' responses to questionnaires. Overall, the limitations are that this approach means it cannot and should not have been treated as solving all problems.

General Issues Arising

The audit approach puts a strong emphasis upon a quantitative survey means of collecting information. This appears particularly helpful where the information required helps in judging an organisation's formalised systems of management development. It provides a quantitative base of argument about management development systems among top managers.

Where a less quantified base for debate and decision-making may be required, then perhaps an alternative, qualitative approach may make more sense. Here, we may be going back more to the development stage of the management development audit itself - that is, better value could come from semi-structured interviews, designed to immerse the researcher in the working experience and problems of managers in the organisation, without pre-defined hypotheses and questions for test. From this process might come the need to check out more systematically the insights that have been gained. However, this could be achieved through detailed conversations with top management and personnel specialists in different businesses. From a researcher's point of view only if there were poor responses to such queries would it be appropriate to consider using a management development audit or similar survey approach.

One final point on choice in collecting data on management development. It is important to note that the role or the relationship of the researcher and clients in the organisation may well be the key to the methods chosen for collecting data. In my own case, investigations could be undertaken as "an insider" rather than an outside consultant. This gave me good access to extensive, informal discussions, without needing necessary permissions or detailed negotiations with clients - as would be required by an outside intervention.

Much of this paper, however, has been around the management development audit and it is perhaps appropriate to finish with comment on that instrument. It would still appear to be quite an attractive and stimulating way to collect data on management development systems. I believe it would also be possible either to see it being used as a regular part of data collection within an organisation, or to use sections of the survey to provide a background of objective information against which specific investigations could be undertaken.

Undoubtedly, the aim of any investigation is to generate data in forms which will be of help to top management decision-makers within the organisation. We know such data can be generated by different means, and it is important for those undertaking such investigations to look at the alternatives and to be sure they have chosen the appropriate methodology.

References

Argyris, C: Intervention Theory and Method, Addison-Wesley, London 1970.

Easterby-Smith, M, Braiden E and Ashton D: Auditing Management Development, Gower Press, London 1980.

Chapter Ten

DETERMINING MANAGEMENT TRAINING NEEDS BY EXAMINING
MANAGEMENT QUALITIES

S Tyson

Introduction

This chapter describes techniques for determining
management training needs, which use a combination of
interview methods and data about individuals gathered
through psychometric tests. Two different
applications are discussed. An "organisation
development" (OD) treatment, where an overall
psychological profile of managers was sought, and a
survey method used to discover managerial
competencies, as a first step in a management
development programme. Both applications address
questions about management qualities. In the former
case, the broad characteristics possessed by a
company's managers, in the latter instance, the
qualities demanded of managers at different levels in
a large public sector organisation.

Training needs analysis

A variety of means exist to determine training needs,
the particular approach being dependent upon whether
analysis is required at an individual or a group
level. This means that where needs are thought to be
common, a group analysis is adopted, for example, by
surveying or through organisation development (OD).
Training needs are also revealed by faults, accidents
or critical incidents which might imply a common
training need. Most typically, the individual level
is seen as appropriate for managers.

Level

	Individual	Individual or Group	Group
Methods	Systems approach	Wastage/faults analysis	Survey methods
	Appraisal schemes	Accidents	OD appro-aches
	Mentoring/ coaching	Critical incidents	

Table 1   Training Needs Analysis

According to the systems approach, training needs are determined by job analysis, where the person specification is used as a basis for selection, and the gap between the requirements described and the attributes of the person selected is the area for improvement, through induction and job related training. The evaluation of that training is fed back to the induction, selection and job analysis stages as a corrective to ensure that the system of selection and training is adjusted to the organisation, and the quality of people passing through the system.

The systems approach is best suited to stable work situations, where there are few changes, where the profile of skills, attitudes and knowledge needed for successful job performance may be taken from the job description. Managerial work is less susceptible to the systems approach because most organisations are subject to change, and those at the most senior levels are more at risk of uncertainty and ambiguity than those in non managerial work, (Mintzberg 1973). Managerial work allows a high degree of discretion and flexibility where personality influences the way the work is done (Stewart 1963, Jaques 1956).

Although in theory, training needs may be discovered from employee appraisals, in practice such data is not always collected, and appraisal schemes may not cover the target populations. More seriously, few appraisal schemes have been validated against any criterion outside the organisation. The measures are highly subjective, and relate only to an internal scale (Fletcher and Williams 1985). Whilst an appraisal scheme may help to adduce the training needs of current jobs, this does not give an understanding of the needs for future jobs, because potential is difficult to judge in the abstract (Stewart and Stewart 1981).

The pace of change facing most organisations now is so rapid that survey methods which are undertaken routinely as part of the change process would seem to be necessary. This is not to deny the utility of "snapshots" of employee attitudes, but rather to suggest that during the overall development of the organisation, opportunities can be taken to "audit" employees in a qualitative way, to judge their current capacity to change, to adapt and to fit into the emerging organisation culture.

The case for a qualitative profile

A qualitative approach is the description one might expect of a survey which is concerned with how people are, what people feel, and with the quality of their relationships. It entails a non experimental design for the survey, which takes a detailed analysis of individual characteristics as the starting point for the discovery of key variables.

Feedback to individuals of data about themselves could be argued to be an essential first step in the process of obtaining individual change. (Nadler 1977). What is required is a thorough, and in-depth feedback of personal data, which shows how the individual relates to his or her group, to the organisation, to the work, and which explores the personality dimensions inherent in individual behaviour. The main concern here is not the personality of the individual, but rather the effect of personality on behaviour. The process of work is thus the main concern: how people achieve tasks, how they adapt, how they act towards their fellows, and how they view themselves.

For management, a qualitative profile of employees is valuable, in order to:

(i)   Audit the fit between the current job and the attributes of the job holder.

(ii)   Provide a basis for career planning and succession arrangements.

(iii)   Reveal trends in the population as a whole, in those dimensions on which measures were taken.

(iv)   Give management a data base on which to plan the future training/development strategy.

The dimensions of an organisational profile

The dimensions chosen for measurement must reflect the philosophy and purposes behind the survey. In the case of managerial work, given the objectives outlined above, evidence would be required on the skills of communication, and analysis, and of the techniques used in gathering and interpreting information, as prerequisites for decision-making. From what many writers have said, the manager's personality strongly influences his or her job; for example, the "process" skills of management (running meetings, negotiation, listening, etc.) are heavily dependent on personality. (McGregor 1960). One may conclude therefore, that the most telling aspects are a description of "personality", of learning style, of the capacity to change, of problem-solving skills, and of what might be described as "managerial" behaviour.

In the following section, one approach to creating an organisational profile is described.

The organisation profiled

This was an old established firm of British printers, which had suffered losses in the recession, due to a very traditional, paternalistic approach to management which had inhibited change. In order to survive the Company sold off its loss-making subsidiaries, invested in new plant and equipment concentrating on one area of the market. A new approach to communications, and major changes at the top of the company helped to introduce a new style of management into this fully unionised company. Real employee involvement was introduced with the unions playing an active part. The new managing director, with the personnel director, convinced their colleagues of the need for a new management philosophy. A large scale training and developmental process was seen as the way to change managerial performance and attitudes. A higher level of management skills was sought, together with improvements in self-confidence, better communication techniques, and more adaptability by managers.

A training programme was thus instigated for around fifty managers over a three year period. The methods used in what was to become a comprehensive development programme included feedback on strengths and weaknesses derived from exercises and psychometric tests, on the job projects, skills training, outdoor development programmes, and team building work with groups of five or six managers at a time. All levels were involved from supervisors to the managing director in all of these developmental activities.

The information for the organisational profile was taken from the data gathered during the first part of the training programme, and from personnel records. In the section that follows there is a brief description of the instruments used to gather the data.

At the start of the training process, the Myers-Briggs questionnaire was introduced as part of the assessment of training needs (Briggs-Myers 1976). At this time, the fundamental issues of individual differences, and different ways of learning were discussed.

From the range of psychometric instruments available, the Myers-Briggs Type Indicator was chosen because of its wide application to career problems, its comprehensive description of adult types on four different axes, producing 16 different categories, and its well-established reputation. The four axes it measures are:

Extraversion	-	Introversion
Sensing	-	Intuition
Thinking	-	Feeling
Judgement	-	Perception

Two other instruments were used. The Thomas-Kilmann conflict mode questionnaire, and the Harrison organisation culture questionnaire were completed immediately prior to a counselling interview conducted with every participating manager, conducted at the end of the first year of the programme.

In the Thomas Kilmann questionnaire, five different approaches towards conflict are determined. (Thomas 1971, 1976). These are:

Competing	:	Forcing, competitive approach, seeking a win-lose position;

Collaborating : Seeking to win, but not at the expense of others;

Compromising : Being prepared to give up a part of one's position, in order to gain some of what one wants;

Avoiding : Not facing the conflict at all;

Accommodating : Allowing the other person to win.

It is argued that there is a repertoire of conflict handling skills, and that the Conflict Mode Instrument indicates which of the five modes the manager uses best, and therefore tends to rely upon. The instrument also examines the mix of modes preferred by that person.

The third instrument was the questionnaire which was developed from Harrison's work on organisation ideologies. (Harrison 1972). Harrison identified four distinct competing organisation ideologies - these are: power orientation, role orientation, task orientation and person orientation.

Power-oriented organisations are autocratic and controlled from the top. Relationships within the organisation are exploitative and aggressive.

Role-oriented organisations are bureaucratic and are slow to react to change. They are rule bound environments, where stability is important.

Task-oriented organisations see achievement and effectiveness as more important than formal authority. There is an "organic" approach to organisation structure, which is seen to be a flexible way of dealing with requirements.

Person-oriented organisations exist only to meet the needs of their members. The emphasis here is on the personal growth and development of the organisation members. The control of organisation members is through persuasion.

In the questionnaire, managers distinguish between how they think their organisation should be classified, and how it appears to be to them. Hence the questionnaire reveals what they think the current organisation culture is, and what they believe it ought to be.

The results of the organisation profile

The outcome from this process is closer to "action learning" than to the more formal survey methods. It is a "problem-centred" approach, where new ideas emerge during the process. A total of 42 managers' profiles were elicited.

The average age of the managers was 41 years, with a spread from 28 to 62 years. They were mostly performing production related jobs as line managers, and there was only a small number of staff in advisory roles (such as the Personnel Manager, and the Work Study officer).

The results of the survey could be summarised as follows: a significant proportion of the management believed in the task ideology. They felt, however, that the organisation had moved to a power culture. These middle managers were typically production oriented, who had been promoted to their current position from the shop floor. Sixteen out of the 41 fell into this category. The majority of these were introverted, sensing, thinking, judging on the Myers-Briggs questionnaire - that is they were: "Practical, orderly, matter-of-fact, logical, realistic, dependable." They lived their outer life more with thinking, inner life more with feeling. However, there was a difference between this group, and those who worked at a higher level, who were either ENTJ (extrovert, intuitive, thinking, judging) or ESTJ (extrovert, sensing, thinking, judging) which is described by Briggs Myers (1976) as:

ENTJ: "Good at anything which requires reasoning and intelligent talk ...... sometimes more confident than their experience warrants".

ESTJ: "Like to organise and run activities". "Practical realists, matter of fact with a natural head for business".

These people were the more senior managers, including the Chief Accountant, and one of the General Managers. Seven of the 41 fell into these two categories of ENTJ or ESTJ. For this group, there was a strong sense of the organisation having a power orientation from the Harrison questionnaire.

When we came to review the results of the Thomas-Kilmann questionnaire, most of the senior managers adopted a "competing" style whereas the ISTJ task oriented production men were collaborative, or compromisers, with the exception of one who tended to "avoid" conflict. The following diagram shows the split graphically. It should be noted, however, that there were a few managers, mostly the staff specialists, who did not fit into this neat dichotomy.

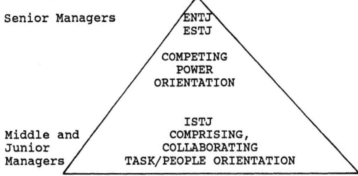

Figure 1   Questionnaire results according to management level

During the course of the counselling interviews, at the end of the first year's programme, this major division in company culture was a cause of concern to the Personnel Director and Managing Director. The problem was expressed as a division between the old style, task-oriented people, and what was perceived to be the new group of senior managers, whose political intrigues and jockeying for position were seen as counter productive.

From the viewpoint of the line production manager, senior staff were enjoying a varied job, with little accountability and a life style of meetings, travel and expenses all paid for by the line manager's activity. This two-cultures revelation was received as a great surprise by senior management.

The consequence of the profile results was to confirm the "fit" between jobs and personality. However, the revelation by the profile that there were few junior managers with a total perspective on management had implications for the career structure of the company, and for its training philosophy. The recruitment policy decision had now to be made of whether or not to go for a two-tier structure of recruitment, or to try and introduce a set of major changes to the training approach.

A survey technique to discover managerial competencies

The second example demonstrates how a simple technique of interviewing managers at different levels, together with data drawn from psychometric tests, helped to discover the managerial competencies required by senior managers at different levels within a large public sector organisation.

The notion of "job competency" has been developed by Klemp (1978) and Boyatzis (1982). A competency is defined as an underlying characteristic of a person through which effective job performance is achieved. Boyatzis argues that there are three facets to a model of effective performance: the individual's competencies, the job's demands, and the organisational environment. Within any description of competencies the type of competency should thus be related to the actions required for effective performance.

Background to the research

The organisation in which the research was conducted was part of the British Civil Service. One requirement of the research was that the results should remain confidential. Accordingly, the Department of State will not be referred to by name, and the description which follows will not mention the results obtained, but will concentrate instead on a discussion of methods.

The British Civil Service has been the subject of a number of reviews which were critical, and which pointed to the absence of adequate managerial training, and argued that the Civil Service had not recognised the importance of a "managerial" function. (Fulton 1968, The English Committee 1976). Management training was seen to be a field where more resources were required. The establishment of a Civil Service College for the training of senior civil servants and the appointment of departmental training officers gave a boost to training.

However, the first priority was technical or job related training, and the training of fast stream administrative trainees. Until recently, there were few signs of a coherent management development strategy. Changes to the organisation of the Civil Service occurred in 1980 after the Conservative government was elected to power. The Civil Service Department was abolished and all central personnel and training responsibilities were moved to the Cabinet Office.

As one part of an overall strategy aimed at improving efficiency within the Civil Service, a Senior Management Development Programme was launched. This was instituted in all Departments for staff at Principal to Under Secretary level, and required managers to make a self assessment against a range of competencies, these being the skills, abilities and knowledge which senior staff were expected to possess. Following their self assessments, managers were required to discuss their own perceptions of competency with their immediate superiors, as a part of the appraisal system. They were then able to select development activities from a menu of training courses, seminars and in-house development activities.

The nature of the managerial competencies had to be investigated before managers could assess themselves, therefore. Whilst it would have been possible to write an arbitrary list, there was a need to determine as precisely as possible what the competencies comprised. Broad headings were drawn up by the Cabinet Office after interviews with top civil servants in all the main departments. However, these interviews were insufficient to cover the specific aspects of each department's work, and it was decided by the departments individually that a more comprehensive list of competencies was needed to augment the headings supplied by the Cabinet Office.

Accordingly, a small research project was commissioned by the department in question, the objective of which was to reflect more accurately departmental needs and priorities. The research described in this paper concerns a project where the competencies of those with the grades of Principal, Senior Principal and Assistant Secretary were to be defined. The department employed around 10,000 people and staff were located at a headquarters and in regional branches.

It is difficult to assign a durable performance standard to all managerial jobs. However, unless a standard is set, it is difficult to measure the training gap, that is the disparity between actual and desired performance. Within the Civil Service, the requirements of the work are clearly defined, but the way the work is done still leaves room for discretion. There may be a number of ways in which work may be accomplished, rather than any one fixed way. Some form of systems approach was appropriate, therefore, but the requirement for understanding different ways of performing was needed. The Cabinet Office, in designing the Senior Management Development Programme had already stressed the value of self assessment and of taking responsibility for one's own learning. This is similar to what Revans has called an action learning approach, where learning is seen as a continuous activity and the chief requirement is for regular and honest feedback from significant others. In the Senior Management Development Programme, training needs were seen as personal, to be met by the individual's own efforts, as well as from the Department's resources.

For this reason an adaptation of the systems approach was attempted, and a training needs analysis method which drew on the perceptions of the job holder seemed to be in accord with the Department's philosophy of training.

Methodology

The methodology adopted followed four stages:

1. The development of a questionnaire, the contents of which were created from the key dimensions described in the jobs at Principal to Assistant Secretary levels. These were the dimensions described in the job description, not the actual work itself, which, as has been stated, varies with individual choice.

    The questionnaire sought information on:

    (a) the main accountabilities

    (b) significant changes in the job recently

    (c) specialist knowledge required

    (d) the main interactions, internally/externally

(e) skills used in performance of role

(f) complexity of the tasks

(g) the analytical skills required

(h) innovative skills required

(i) decision-making level

(j) the training needed to perform effectively

(k) the education required to perform effectively

(l) the experience required to perform effectively

These were defined, and examples were given of each area, to be quoted at the interview.

2. Interviews were conducted with a representative sample, randomly drawn, of Principals, Senior Principals, and Assistant Secretaries. The sampling frame was designed to cover all the main areas of work, in the department and an appropriate balance between HQ and the Regions. The grades covered were represented according to the percentage in the total population.

Assistant Secretaries:	9
Senior Principals:	7
Principals:	21
Total:	37

Each interview lasted approximately one-and-a-half hours and was conducted in private at the premises of the interviewee. Although the interviews followed the schedule, ample scope was given for fruitful lines of enquiry.

3. The interviewees were given the Myers Briggs test to discover any relationship between personality or cognitive style, and the competencies.

Triangulation of the data

The interviews conducted in this case were used to attempt to "triangulate" the data, by comparing the results from the managers interviewed, across the categories. This triangulation serves to eliminate bias although of course the result is a collection of visions, rather than one authoritatively "correct" account.

One type of comparison was hierarchical between:

    Assistant Secretary
    Senior Principal
    Principal

with reports of the competencies being produced by each of the managers, both on subordinates, superiors, and on self.

The second comparison was horizontal:

    Assistant Secretary   Assistant Secretary
    Senior Principal   Senior Principal
    Principal   Principal

when they were asked to comment on their current work as typical of the kind found at that level. The results were also sorted by grade, in order to collect the data together.

The policy of promoting and moving civil servants through many different posts provides each person with a range of experience which can be a valuable source of data on all jobs. Formal quantitative measures are not always necessary when examining a group of people who belong to a homogeneous culture, where direct observations and interviewing can reveal the repeating patterns of behaviour which are the norm for the population. Civil servants in this sense are more like a primitive group or tribe, where once the codes of behaviour have been discovered, a range of actions becomes meaningful. The civil servants interviewed belonged to a homogeneous subculture, where a relatively small sample can reveal a whole pattern. (Barton and Lazarsfeld 1955).

Conclusion to the competencies project

The approach outlined in this project is a standard one in that job analysis usually requires an interview of the job holder. However, the attempt both to triangulate the data, and to investigate the findings from the psychometric test adds validity to the findings, as a perception of the reality of managerial work at senior levels within the Department which such senior staff would recognise. The research produced a list of 66 particular competencies, with detailed descriptions of the skills, knowledge, techniques necessary for performance of these competencies. From the psychometric results the common characteristics of the subjects were shown to be a highly critical and evaluative, practical approach. This was in keeping with the duties of the staff in their early work, as junior staff. However, the unimaginative aspects of the profile were not likely to be helpful at more senior levels.

Self assessment of training needs requires the researcher to use the words of the interviewees as much as possible, and to discover their way of thinking, so that managers can match their own perceptions of their strengths and weaknesses against a list which is understandable.

Concluding summary

In this paper I have tried to show how management training needs may be analysed at the organisational level. In the first example, it was argued that the assessment of training needs can be undertaken as a first step in the development process, so that through feedback and discussion, learning for the trainers and for the training population occurs. From the aggregation of this data came a new perspective on the organisation as a whole. The profile showed the training strategy in a new light, and raised important questions about recruitment policy, and the organisation's culture.

The second example described an approach where the training population's views of the competencies required were established as a necessary first step to a development programme. The competencies for managerial work are clearly dependent on the manager's personality characteristics and the interpersonal skills demanded by the tasks they are expected to perform. The increasing pace of change means many managers face unstructured and often unforeseen demands, day by day, to which only the most general competency can therefore be attached.

191

It can be argued that there are no such things as "jobs", but there are people in jobs. Jobs do not have a physical existence. Although there are tasks which one may envisage, the collection of these tasks into "jobs" requires a conceptualisation on the part of the person who is thinking of the "job". Translating this concept into a different realm of reality, where people actually perform the tasks, requires a leap into the world of personality, feelings and individual capacities. From both these examples, one may see that simple survey methods exist for the analysis of training needs which allow for the move from one level of reality to the other.

References

Barton, A H and Lazarsfeld, P F: Some Functions on
     Qualitative Analysis in Social Research.
     Frankfurter Beitrage zur Sociologie 1985.   Vol. 1
     pp 321-361.

Boyatzis, R E: The Competent Manager.   A Model of
     Effective Performance.   John Wiley   1982.

Briggs-Myers, I: Introduction to Type.   Centre for
     Applications of Psychological Type. Florida 1976.

Fletcher, C: and Williams, R: Performance Appraisal
     and Career development.   Hutchinson 1985.

Harrison, R: Understanding your organisation's
     character.   Harvard Business Review 1972.

Jaques, E: Measurement of Responsibility. Tavistock
     1956.

Nadler, D A: Feedback and OD using data-based methods.
     Addison Wesley 1977.

Klemp, G O: JR Job Competence Assessment. Boston McBer
     1978.

McGregor, D: The Human Side of Enterprise.   McGraw
     Hill 1960.

Mintzberg, H: The Nature of Managerial Work.   Harper
     and Row 1973.

Stewart, A and Stewart, V: Tomorrow's Managers Today.
     Institute of Personnel Management   1981.

Stewart, R: The Reality of Management.   Pan   Piper
     1963.

Thomas, K: Conflict and Conflict Management in M.D.
     Dunnette (Ed) Handbook of Industrial and
     Organisational Psychology pp 889-935 University of
     Minnesota.   John Wiley 1976.

Thomas, K: Conflict-handling modes in inter-
     departmental relations. Unpublished doctoral
     thesis Prudence University Indianna 1971.

Expenditure (General sub committee) The 'English'
    Committee Minutes of House of Commons Evidence
    HMSO 1976.

Fulton Report Committee on the Civil Service Vol 1.
    Report Conrad 3638 HMSO 1968.

Chapter Eleven

METHODS USED IN THE SURVEY OF MANAGEMENT CAREER
PLANNING: A NORWEGIAN PROJECT IN ACTION RESEARCH

P Joynt

Introduction

The concept of surveying is very closely related to
the concept of methodology in the traditional research
paradigm:

> Problem

> Theory

> Methodology

> Analysis

> Conclusions

In this paper we will look at the methodology
strategies used in attempting to study the behaviour
involved in a management career. The context is that
of Norway, and the project involves the Norwegian
Employers' Confederation as well as the following
companies studying the career behaviour of managers
who move out of management positions:

Esso	Moller (VW of Norway)
Shell	Elkem
STK (ITT of Norway)	Actinor
Philips	Elekstrisk Bureau
Sparebanken	Philips
Den norske Creditbank	Selmer/Sande
Borregaard	

The research part of the project is coordinated by the Institute for Management Research at the Norwegian School of Management in Oslo.

The concept of career planning, like the concept of organisational specialisation, is a popular target of criticism. It prompts us immediately to dwell on the Chaplin man on the assembly line, defenceless, monotonised, dehumanised for a lifetime. Planned specialisation or job design serves to define the boundaries between organisation jobs, so that the need for coordination is reduced to an appropriate level. The "appropriate" level often involves a trade-off between the organisational demands and needs for the processing of resources and the individual's abilities, needs and energy level.

Much of the recent work on contingency theory has added a dynamic orientation to today's practice, since it involves organisations and managers reacting to a constantly changing environment. Likewise, much of the study on the psychology of man has involved a realisation that a person's abilities, needs and energy levels change as a function of time. This is particularly true for management jobs, which is the main focus of this research. Our emphasis is not on the theory or the results of the research, but rather on the methodologies used in studying career behaviour for managers of different ages. Since the research uses action learning as a central ideology, it was essential to describe the "existing" situation prior to moving into the dynamics of the challenge of matching individuals to organisations and jobs over a lifetime.

The Existing Situation at the Organisation Level of Analysis

In any action research design a certain amount of resources are necessary to describe the situation as it exists now. In the project reported on here, this work involved a group of interviews with each of the companies mentioned previously. Some fifteen organisational working hypotheses were involved. These hypotheses ranged from company use of courses on career planning to the amount of individual information the company kept on the financial situation for each manager - health status, family status, etc.

The interviews were conducted on a trial basis in two of the companies by a research team involving three members. The interview was conducted with the personnel director and/or a team from the personnel department. This initial interview was conducted at the company, and lasted from two to four hours. Supplementary information was provided in the form of annual reports, company newspapers and minutes of key meetings the company might have had on career planning. Often a three to four page report was made by one of the researchers, summarising the interview and subsequent information.

The two trial runs were necessary to test both the companies' interpretation of the hypotheses as well as the researcher's interpretation. Since a research team of three was used and some of the hypotheses had a subjective tone, it was important that all parties were in general agreement here. Interestingly enough, several of the hypotheses were revised because of:

new information from the companies

new subjective interpretations from the researchers

new subjective interpretations from the company representatives

feedback from other researchers who had worked in this area

One might argue that one is dealing with a degree of uncertainty (March and Olsen 1982), even at this preliminary phase in the research process.

In addition, there is often a dichotomy between theory and the real world, which it is impossible to reduce to a minimum without a few iterations. This would thus suggest that one compromises the traditional research strategy shown in Table 1.

Table 1: The Traditional Step by Step Approach to Hypothesis

Testing

1. Formulate problem area   5. Select sample size
2. Search for relevant theory   6. Write results
3. Trial test
4. Revision made

Figure 1: The Deductive Spiral Approach to Hypothesis
          Testing

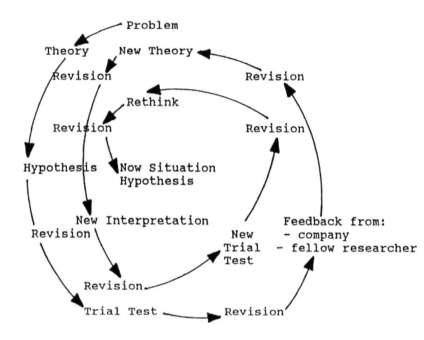

A more appropriate description of the process that was
actually used is shown in Figure 1, where a type of
deductive spiral (Cattell 1966) is used and revision
is commonplace. Using the deductive spiral approach,
the research team adopted the phrase "working
hypothesis" to underline the changing nature of their
work at this descriptive now-oriented phase of the
research project.

Upon completion of the initial interviews, a matrix
was constructed interfacing each company result with
the "now" situation working hypothesis being tested.
This matrix contained both objectives as well as
subjective information, and the researchers attempted
to answer each hypothesis with a qualified yes or a
qualified no as well as subjective comments and
objective information. The matrix map allowed the
research team to get a better view of the "now
situation", using the sample of ten companies. The
matrix map (shown below) was then used as the prime

document for writing the research report that
summarised this phase of the project (Johnsen and
Joynt 1984).

Matrix Map	C1	C2	C3	C4	C5	C6	C7	C8	C9	C10
Hypothesis 1										
Hypothesis 2										
Hypothesis 3										
Hypothesis 15										

C = Company

Figure 2: Matrix Map

The report was written using the matrix as the prime
document, supplemented by the more detailed folder on
each company. The method used to generate the final
report, was a modified version of content analysis
(Wood 1984). Daft (1983) suggests that a qualitative,
rather than quantitative style is more appropriate
where the results of hypothesis testing involve
complex behaviours. This approach was adopted, and an
added emphasis was placed on unique findings. The
main reason for this emphasis on the unique finding –
in, say, one or two companies - was to motivate and
inform the other companies so that a type of dynamic
exchange of ideas could start. Here the aspect of
action research enters (Revans 1983), where one of the
major goals is to exchange current views and practices
among companies as well as individuals, and the
companies thus begin to adopt each other's practices.

Upon completion of the working paper summarising the
"now situation" at the organisational level, the
research team circulated a draft of the report to the
companies involved. The confidentiality of each
company was maintained, as the report used only
integrated general information. The "unique"
situations were disguised, or the company(ies)
involved authorised publication of their practice.
Another interview was held with each company in order
to gain feedback on the working paper draft as well as

a final check on the results of the first interview. This second interview and feedback session was held at the Management Research Institute. It may be a minor technicality, but the first interviews involved obtaining information, and the company location was the logical choice. The second interview involved checking information which the Research Institute had processed, and, thus, the natural choice was the Institute location. In summary, a new spiral of feedback and revisions was used after completion of an initial working paper draft on the results of testing the working hypotheses. The entire process involved approximately one year before the final report was published.

The Existing Situation at the Individual Level

Much of the research in the career planning area has focused on the individual level of analysis. Schein (1978) used interviews with approximately 50 MBA graduates in finding his well-known career anchors. Bartolome and Evans (1980) also used interviews on a group of European managers. Hedaa (1978) used questionnaires on some 1,200 managers to test both individual and organisational hypotheses. Finally, Joynt (1983) used a questionnaire on managers from some twenty Norwegian companies. From the above, we might conclude that the interview and questionnaire are the two most common methodologies in studying individual career planning behaviour. Perhaps behaviour is not the correct concept, since much of the work involves a testing of attitude hypothesis. However, for our purposes we assume that attitudes, beliefs, motives and needs are part of the broad concept of individual career related behaviour.

In this area of the project, a traditional questionnaire was used for two reasons. First, the team was interested in sampling a broad range of managers, and the questionnaire proved to be the least expensive of the alternatives available. Second, the team was interested in building on the results of prior research in the career planning area, thus the bias was towards testing rather well-known concepts and hypotheses using the Norwegian context.

After a half year's work, a six pages questionnaire was pretested on a sample of 80 managers (Mohr 1984). The respondents were encouraged to "help" us develop a questionnaire that could be understood by the average manager. As such, there was space designed for comments built into the questionnaire. The team also found that the best results were obtained when a group of individuals could be assembled and introduced to the questionnaire. Several companies found that a lunch period was often a good opportunity to assemble a small group. Practicing managers attending classes at the Norwegian School of Management, were also used. Again a meal period was used, where the participants were encouraged to use part of their evening meal for the project. Response rates outside of planned group activities averaged about 50% as opposed to over 80% when a group session was used.

Data from 60 individual managers was used in this pre-testing phase. Close to half of them had detailed comments which assisted the researchers in making the necessary revisions. Once the revisions were made, the questionnaire was again trial-tested with a small group of five managers. Here, feedback was obtained immediately after completion of the questionnaire. The final questionnaire is currently written in Norwegian only. It contains a variety of questionnaire techniques which include ranging, checking and appropriate box comments sections and drawing a diagram. The bulk of the questionnaires will be processed through normal computer methods. However, the comments and diagram sections will be processed by hand. Since the project involves ten companies as well as plans for including other organisations and other nations in a future comparative study, a data strategy was required. The strategy involved the following classification division:

Unit	1	Company	1	
"	2	Company	2	
"	3	Company	3	
"	4	Company	4	
"	5	Company	5	ACTION RESEARCH
"	6	Company	6	PROJECT *
"	7	Company	7	
"	8	Company	8	
"	9	Company	9	
"	10	Company	10	
"	11	Company	11	
"	12	Company	12	
"	13	Company	13	Other Norwegian
				Organisations
"	14	Company	14	Country 2
"	15	Company	15	Country 3
"	16	Company	16	Country 4

"	17	Company	17	Country	5
"	18	Company	18		

* An eleventh company was added in November 1984, and a number twelve in December 1984, so the Action Research project involves 12 companies.

This strategy allows, again, for the comparision of results between the companies. In addition, a large group of some 100 Norwegian organisations will be integrated into the data base in 1986. Here the data on each organisation will not be registered, but rather put into a single unit in the files. The first eleven units then represent the Norwegian sample for the individual level of analysis, and are filed by organisation unit.

Heller (in Joynt and Warner 1984) points to the difficulty of conducting conmparative or cross cultural research because of the costs, opportunities, languages and cultures involved. Despite this, he and others point to the need for a larger concentration in this area. This study will thus add an international dimension in 1986, which will include adapting (translating included) the questionnaires for other nations. Since much of the initial career research work has Anglo-Saxon origins, the translation into English/American should be minor. However, a good deal of work will be required for other countries outside Scandinavia.

The research plan thus involves using the <u>individual</u> questionnaires:

in an organisational context (Units 1-12)

in an international context (Units 1-12 plus Units 13 -18)

in a general context (Units 1-18)

Numerous other strategies were available which could have included:

- remaining at the individual level of analysis

- using only a Norwegian organisational level of analysis

-       using the above two in each country

Ultimately, the research decisions are often a combination of research opportunities and the finanacial realities of the situation.

This paper will not go into detail concerning the different statistical techniques that could be used. It is expected that these will grow as the data bank grows, and will very much depend on the research problem at the moment. As an example of this, unemployment is a major problem for most countries, and the interest in the project often stems from this initial problem definition. Perhaps in the future, the problem will be the right to a job for life, or the need for limited periods of time in very challenging management jobs. The questionnaire may need to be adjusted so as to incorporate these new realities. Here validity and reliability play a major role in the trade-offs involved. The over-emphasis on quantitative techniques and their associated tendency towards a conservative view on changing the contents of a questionnaire, is a central focus in many of the organisation behaviour journals of today. One of the major factors in the debate includes staying current. The experience in this project shows that a great deal of time has been spent defending the results of the past and moving in the "duplication" direction rather than including, building and changing based on the realities of today.

The contents of the questionnaire and the statistical and computer strategies are also items that require a great deal of pre-planning in the area of methodology. Here the trade-off is often between user (practitioner) understanding and academic publication. At present, the project has a heavy bias towards user understanding, not so much in the normative (cook book) direction, but rather in the direction of "Here's some interesting preliminary results, can you use them?" or "What do you need to proceed further?".

Researching our own behaviour as researchers we found the above were some of our major problems. Unfortunately, the present literature has spent all too little time in these areas.

A few good cases so that the many may follow (learn)

Many people fault behavioural science or organisational behaviour research for being too concerned with description and understanding and not enough concerned with control or normative action. In this phase of the research, our goal, moves from a description of the existing "now situation" towards an action research and learning emphasis. Here we are interested not only in the learning dimensions of description and understanding, but also in a subtle normative action. In many respects, we are interested in spreading the good word so that others may follow.

One of the major goals of the project, as stated in the research proposal to the Norwegian Employers' Confederation (NAF), was to gain acceptance for management behaviour involving moving out of key senior responsibilities prior to the normal retirement age. An additional perspective closely related to this goal, was to find out the attitudes of managers about retirement age. In Norway the "normal" retirement age is 67 years - some prefer this age, others a lower age and still others feel a person has a right to a job as long as (s)he wishes.

The temptation to "make" theory prior to the study of practice is great when the academic is faced with this type of problem. In this project, the research team elected to find and study the few situations where a manager had moved out of a top job, and document them as case studies. Each company was asked if they had examples of this, and the result was a group of approximately 30 managers who, for some reason, had moved out of very responsible management positions.

The next phase involved a very open interview where the person in question was asked to relate his or her feelings and experiences connected to the career move mentioned above. The interview guideline is shown below:

Constructive management mobility

Often it is difficult for managers to develop life long career plans because so much is outside their direct control. Others control the access to jobs, promotion, success, status and time for reduction of job responsibility.

On the other hand, few take the time to evaluate their own priorities, personal strengths and weaknesses. The Norwegian Employers Association along with the Management Research Institute at the Norwegian School of Management are interested in studying the behaviour associated with management career paths. We are interested in the career paths and roles of managers over 40 years of age. We need more knowledge about the attitudes of older managers in roles such as counsellor, mentor, coordinator and top manager. We are particularly interested in managers who have experienced a reduction in job responsibility prior to retirement.

We would like you to map the career changes you have made, emphasising the relationship between the demands of a management job on the one hand and your own competence, energy and value priorities on the other. Other factors closely associated with the above are health, family status, financial issues, hobbies, pension and other age insurance.

Would you take the time to map your own behaviour and experiences in this area? We suggest a three to five pages report which will be treated as confidential if you so wish. We can also assist in typing and editing the report. Some of the reports will be translated into Norwegian for further use in the project.

We sincerely appreciate your taking the time to share this key life experience with us, and hope it will provide aid to others who face career decisions and would benefit from your insights.

> Thank you for your
> time and interest.

Note: The original is in Norwegian.

These guidelines were used on a sample of 20 Norwegian managers. In addition, some 10-15 managers from English speaking countries have been asked to submit a five pages case history of their experience using the guidelines shown.

The research group intends to conduct approximately twenty interviews, using the open interview guide shown above. Upon completion of this pre-testing phase, a more structured interview guide will be made incorporating:

The key concepts found in the open structured pre-tests on twenty managers.

Previous theory, Schein's career anchors are an example here.

The information needs of the companies.

At this point the goal is to obtain as many cases (examples) as possible. As such, both interviews and solicited written cases will be used. In soliciting a case, the prospect will be sent a rather structured questionnaire with some open-ended questions. In addition (s)he will be asked to write a three to five pages case on their own experience using their own words, values and attitudes.

The above information and cases will form the main aspect of the action research strategy. We are interested in teaching other managers through the first-hand experience documents produced in this phase. The theory produced must be "user friendly" (Sheldon 1973) or involve "walking stick" theory (Henderson 1979), so that the manager interested in making a career move can take the necessary action based on the information (s)he has obtained from the project.

The action research project perspective from a methodology point of view

Revans (1983) divides action learning into two learning dimensions: a learning dimension based on school learning where concepts, definitions, history and theories are central; the second dimension emphasising some type of learning from trial and error, in other words from experience. In most behaviours, both are necessary and tend to supplement and complement one another. This is particularly true with management behaviour, where the school practice debate has raged for years. The solution is not one of either/or, but rather one of integration. This is particularly true with the problem (or opportunity) being studied here - that of management career mobility.

One of the major tenets in action research and learning is that people learn from one another, and can often assist one another in the solving of problems. In career mobility for managers, we are often talking about an infinity of cases and variables, yet somehow certain concepts or processes emerge. Schein used the concept "career anchors" after extensive interviews with MBA students. Psychologists use the concept "phases of life" to illustrate the changing human nature in all of us.

In the action research process mentioned here, we are not only interested in presenting previous concepts and theories, but also in presenting first-hand knowledge about Norwegian managers who have experienced a major change in their career path. We are interested in documenting as much of this information as possible, so that others may learn by it.

As was mentioned, the situations may be infinite: the military officer who moves into a personnel director position; the managing director who moves into a consultant position; the marketing director who starts his own consulting firm; the production manager who turns to farming; the research director who becomes a professor; the administrative director who becomes a politician. The variety of cases could go on and on, but some type of feelings and processes may emerge when it is all sorted out. This is the researcher's job in an action learning perspective. The job is a complex one, because it involves the dissemination of information intended to create further actions by another manager who can learn from the cases and information at hand. The researcher in the final analysis must act as the middle person between a dynamic, changing theory and the needs of a manager wishing to make a career change.

The researcher's role becomes one of mapping the changes that occur in the 12 organisations involved. This is accomplished by using a variety of qualitative methods such as: meeting summaries, cases, open-ended interviews with key actors, documentation from planned meetings with the 12 organisations as well as quantitative data such as number of five year contracts, number of managers who move out of these positions, part time arrangements etc.

At present one could diagram the status of the project as follows:

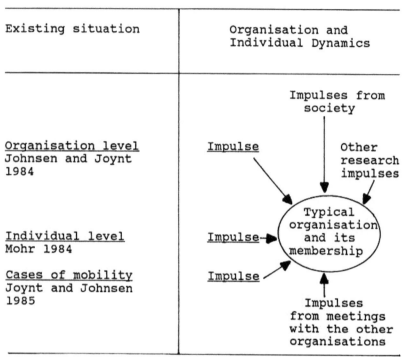

Existing situation	Organisation and Individual Dynamics

Figure 3: Research level and research dyamics

Conclusions

The methodology section in most research reports is a short section usually involving a standard statistical package with some attention to validity and reliability. In an action research and learning perspective, the methodology issues often are the focal point. It is here major issues involving the further dissemination of information gathered by the researchers is not primarily used to document evidence of some particular theory of behaviour for other researchers, but rather to suggest alternative career patterns for practicing managers. Here the issues of validity and reliability are often replaced by relevance and a subtle learning strategy. One is spreading the good word to practitioners rather than to fellow researchers. One expects a career behaviour response from academia. This by no means suggests that this interaction should possibly come at a later stage in the research project. Here the entire action learning perspective can be accounted for by answering questions such as:

What was learned by those managers involved?

What individual actions took place?

What organisational actions took place?

What were the consequences of the above three questions in terms of behavioural theory?

In conclusion, this paper suggests that for some behavioural problems new research reporting strategies are necessary, emphasising the need to look at methodology more pragmatically, where the needs of all parties are considered and documented.

> "It is a capital mistake to theorise before one has data".
>
> Sir Arthur Conan Doyle

I wish to thank Paul Johnsen, Erling Bjordal, Kristin Watle and Morten Mohr for their assistance in making the project and, thus, this paper possible. Implied in "these" thanks are the 12 organisations who are directly involved in action learning.

References

Bartolome, F and Revans, P: Must Success cost so much? Harvard Business Review March/April 1980.

Bjordal, E: Konstruktiv ledermobilitet. Arbeid og laering 1/84.

Cattell, R B: Handbook of Multivariate Experimental Psychology. Chicago: Rand McNally 1966.

Daft, R L: Organisation Theory and Design. New York: West 1983.

Hedaa, L: Den aeldre leders karrieresituasjon. Copenhagen: I.P. Press 1979.

Heller, F: From Managing in Different Cultures. Joynt and Warner (eds.). Oslo: Universitetsforlaget 1984.

Henderson, L J: On the Social System: Selected Writings. Chicago: Chicago University Press 1970.

Johnsen, P and Joynt, P: Management Mobility in Ten Norwegian Companies. EIASM Conference on New Challenges for Management, Leuven 1984.

Joynt, P: Decruitment: A New Personnel function. International Studies of Management Organisation XII (3), 1983

Joynt, P: Research-Based Projects as a Learning Strategy in Business Schools. Human Relations 36, 1983.

March, J and Olsen, J P: Ambiguity and Choice in Organisations. Oslo: Universitetforlaget 1982.

Mohr, M: A Pilot Study of Attitudes to Moving out of Key Management Positions before Pensioning. Masters Thesis. Brunel University 1984.

Revans, R: ABC of Action Learning. Kent: Chartwell-Bratt 1983.

Schein, E: Career Dynamics. Reading, Mass: Addison-Wesley 1978.

Sheldon, A: Friendly Models. Science, Medicine and Man 1973.

Skinner, B F: Intellectual Self-Management in Old Age.
    American Psychologist March 1983.

Sonnenfeld, J: Dealing with the Aging Work Force.
    Harvard Business Review. No./Dec. 1978.

Wood, S: Content Analysis as a Research Methodology.
    1984.

Chapter Twelve

ANALYSING INCENTIVE PAYMENT SYSTEMS

A Bowey

Introduction

This chapter focuses on the issues involved in
studying the effects of deliberately introduced
changes in the methods used by an organisation to
calculate how much pay their employees are to receive.
The basis for these considerations derives from a
study of incentive payment systems introduced in 63
different employing organisations (Bowey, Thorpe and
Hellier 1986). The aim of that study was to identify
the factors which influenced the success or otherwise
of these schemes. How important to eventual results
were such things as the design features of the payment
system itself, the suitability of the payment system
for the kind of organisation it was introduced into,
the kind of organisation itself, and the processes
through which the changes were implemented?

Several different models of the way these causal
influences might be operating were devised and tested.
Figure 1 shows these various models in diagrammatic
form. The arrows represent possible causal links.

The first model (row (a) in Figure 1) postulates a
commonly held view amongst many managers even today,
that certain types of payment system are better than
others. It is because of this view that we have
experienced the fashions in incentive payment systems
with direct work-measured individual incentive schemes
being superceded first by measured day-work, then by
added value schemes, and more recently by gainsharing
schemes. According to model (a), the type of payment
system produces the results; in other words, the
nature of the structural change being introduced
produces changes in the organisation's performance.

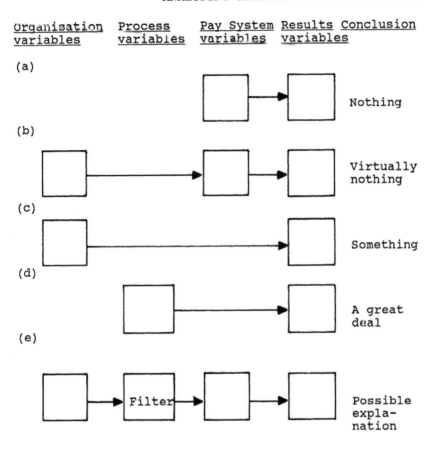

Figure 1: Alternative models of causal influences on payment system resulsts

To test this theory proved more difficult than expected, because payment systems do not fall easily into types (in spite of the impression given in the literature). They vary in numerous ways, and the names which are used for them are often more misleading than helpful in understanding what the features of a scheme are.

We used various statistical and logical ways of combining payment system features into categories which could then be used for classifying the systems themselves; but the results of testing these categories against variables measuring the results of the changes were poor. We found the most useful way of analysing the effects of different payment systems was to consider specific features of schemes separately, and test whether they correlated with any of the results variables.

Pay System Variables

The pay system variables used for this purpose included the following:

How often was the incentive or bonus paid?
Did the scheme require work study?
What kind of action earned extra pay (eg. more out put, effort, quality, etc.)?
Was the scheme based on individual or group performance?
Was the extra payment a fixed or a variable amount?
How large a proportion of total pay was it?
How easy or complicated was the calculation of extra pay?

The second problem with assessing the effects of these schemes, was to decide how to judge results. In particular there were wide discrepancies in expectations from the schemes. Were they expected to improve financial performance, were they expected to reduce unit costs and so reduce inflation (the government of the day's hope), were they intended to assist the organisation in overcoming some problems it was facing and with which its employees could help, or were they just a way of paying the employees more money? All of these aims were expressed to us by some people, and sometimes all from within the same organisation.

We overcame this problem by using a long list of result variables, and assessing whether the variables we were testing correlated closely with any of the result variables. In this way we could find out what the changes had produced, and leave the judgement of whether these were beneficial changes until a later stage. We could also assess whose aims had been most closely achieved by the new payment systems.

The result variables which we used for these purposes included the following:

Result Variables

Output	Overtime
Profit	Punctuality
Productivity	Differentials
Flexibility	Manning
Costs	Machine utilisation
Quality	Safety
Effort	Breakdown time
Absence	Morale
Wastage	Cooperation
Relationships	Rejects
Comments on the organisation	Delivery
Earnings	Prices

When the pay system variables were tested against these result variables no close correlations were found. This was no surprise to our team, because organisation studies have, for many years, been informing managers that there are no panacea solutions in management; no structural change such as a type of payment system is going to produce consistently favourable results irrespective of where and how it is introduced.

The literature on organisation theory suggests that features of the organisation and its context affect the results, and these must be taken into account in trying to understand the results of an intervention or in trying to plan one with a particular aim in mind. This point of view has been labelled "Contingency Theory". Contingency theory (in its various forms) contests that the results of an intervention (such as a change of payment system) in an organisation are dependent upon the characteristics of the organisation as well as the nature of the intervention (Lupton 1975, Legge 1979).

Depending upon the particular form of contingency theory espoused, this is either taken to mean that organisations will only survive and prosper if they match their internal structure to the contingent requirements of their situation; or to mean that by choosing to match their internal structure to the contingent requirements of their situation, people in organisations can improve the organisation's performance. Contingency theory is represented by model (b) in Figure 1.

In order to test this theory one needs a variety of different organisations introducing different forms of the particular structural change being examined (in this case, the payment system). The organisational context was measured by means of a wide range of organisational variables, which had been identified from the organisation theory literature and from previous studies of payment systems as being potentially relevant to the way in which an intervention, such as a new payment system, was likely to operate. They included the following:

Organisational Variables

Size
Market saturation
Investment plans
Rate of technological change
Order completion time
Skill levels
Measurement of effort
Importance of quality
Automation vs operator control of speed
Repetitiveness of work
Calibre of supervision
Span of control
Previous pay system
Locus of bargaining
Type of technology
Management education
Region
Industry
Objectives
Levels of pay
Use of method study.

These variables were important to any attempt to test the contingency theory approach to analysing the results. The type of the intervention was measured through the payment system variables, and it was then possible to assess whether the association between the payment system variables and the result variables was stronger in some circumstances than in others. This was done by holding constant each of the organisational variables in turn, and then in combination, whilst correlating pay system variables with result variables.

The outcome was very disappointing, in the sense that very few improvements were found in the correlations, and in some cases the relationship was much weakened under certain contextual conditions, indicating that the original relationship was explained by both variables correlating with the test factor (i.e. both the payment system feature and the result were more common in that kind of organisational situation than in others).

This led our team to examine the relationships between the organisational variables themselves and the result variables, model (c) in Figure 1. In a number of cases, the link between organisation feature and results was stronger than either the links between payment systems and results or these same links when organisation features were held constant. For example, organisations with a low market saturation had managed to increase their volume of output better than other organisations, irrespective of the kind of payment systems they had introduced.

It would appear from this that contingency theory as defined by these tests was not supported by the results. In other words, it is not the case that good results will be obtained from a payment system provided it is designed to be suited to the particular organisation into which it is introduced.

The next test in our study was to look at process variables, to assess whether an explanation of the differences in results obtained (and these were very considerable between organisations) could be found there (model d in Figure 1). In truth, by this stage we were becoming anxious that none of our tests explained the results, and were testing every variable we had data on to find the ones which did explain the results.

Process Variables

The process variables which were tested included the following:

1. Who was involved in negotiation of the scheme?
2. Who was involved in consultation about the scheme?
3. How well did departments understand the scheme?
4. Time spent in negotiation
5. Time spent in consultation
6. Adequacy of information about negotiation and consultation
7. Adequacy of explanation of the scheme
8. Time spent explaining the scheme
9. Whether method study had been used as part of the implementation
10. Whether work measurement was used
11. Whether financial data was used in designing the scheme
12. What staff were assigned to monitor the scheme
13. Did staff increase to implement scheme
14. Whether management was required to collect more information
15. Whether time standards were prepared for the scheme.

When these variables were tested against the result variables it was found that some of them correlated substantially better with good results than any of the variables tested earlier. In particular the first eight, which all related to the process of negotiation and consultation about the scheme, correlated closely, and when a composite variable was devised combining scores on these eight variables, this was by far the best explanation of the differences between organisations' results from their new payment system.

The key result of this extensive four-year study was, then, that organisations which had spent more time and effort in constructive consultation about their new payment scheme before its introduction had experienced the greatest benefits from the changes they had introduced. This was true irrespective of the kind of scheme they had introduced and the kind of situation into which it was introduced. Our original dilemma about which result variables were most valid turned out to be unimportant because such a large number of the result variables correlated positively with consultation, and with hardly anything else.

It is worth mentioning that the study did produce some useful information about features of payment systems which correlated positively with benefits though not statistically significantly so. In other words, we learned that certain features had a higher probability than others of leading to beneficial results, although they were by no means guaranteed to do so in all circumstances. These features included such things as group-based rather than individual performance-based schemes; providing tight and explicit specifications of the work to be done to earn the extra pay; and bonus or incentive pay which varies with the performance as opposed to being a fixed extra payment. More details of the statistics and methodology of this study are to be found in Bowey et al. 1982 and 1986.

The first results of this study became available in 1981, and at about that time a marine engine building company named Kincaid's approached us for assistance in the design of an incentive payment system. They were informed of the results of the study, and told that the way to improve organisational performance via an incentive scheme was to embark upon a process of consultation about the proposal before its implementation. This was a major change of style for the company, but was consistent with the preferred approach of the newly appointed production manager and the new managing director who joined the company shortly afterwards.

The aims of the consultation were defined as being to identify the key areas for improvement in the company, to relate these to some feasible objectives for the new incentive payment system, to ensure everyone in the company was familiar with the aims of the project and of the new incentive scheme, to ensure commitment to the aims of the scheme before its introduction, and to involve the entire management and workforce in designing and using the incentive payment system as a means of improving the company's performance.

This company was experiencing very serious problems at the time this work began. Figure 2 shows some of the more serious of them, as identified by a management team which began the project. There was a very poor physical layout of the two sites, which were a quarter of a mile apart along a busy main road, with production being split between them in an ill-planned way, and large engine components being ferried by crane and lorries backwards and forwards for the various operations to be carried out on them. A calculation indicated that some components travelled eight miles between entering the works and eventually leaving it on an engine.

The next problem was that very high levels of overtime were being worked, in spite of the fact that this company was short of work due to the state of the industry generally and its own poor reputation for quality and delivery in particular. Morale was very low due to the constant fear of closure and redundancy, and many managers felt it would be impossible to motivate the workforce in these circumstances. Indeed that was part of the rationale for wishing to introduce an incentive payment system, to provide the motivation which was otherwise lacking. There was very poor, almost non-existent production control and the same was true of the financial control system. The skills of both management and workforce were outdated in terms of the needs of a company seeking to compete in this very tough declining industry. And there was a section of the work which had been lost to this company some years ago, with a workforce which was completing the outstanding work before being made redundant. These redundancies were proceeding very slowly, and here again it was hoped that an incentive payment system would motivate the men to finish the work faster.

As a result of these problems, the company was taking far too long to complete the orders for engines which it did attract (at the time a ship could be completed in nine months, but Kincaid's would quote thirteen months for the engine); on top of this they then consistently took longer than the contract allowed to complete the work, and were delivering on average six months late; and added to that their costs of manufacturing these engines was substantially higher than the price at which the same engines could be bought elsewhere in Europe.

Taken together these factors did spell doom for the company, and we were given the information some time later that the original intention had been to introduce an incentive scheme to persuade the workforce to complete their outstanding orders, and then to close down the company. However, we did not know this, and set about trying to involve people from all levels in the company in a consultative system to identify the areas which needed improvement, and to design an incentive scheme to reward the workforce for contributing to these improvements.

The system for consultation took the form of small groups at departmental level which cut across the levels in the company, and which met regularly to discuss how their department could contribute to the organisational priorities. These groups were named "Productivity Circles", an unfortunate name because many people subsequently confused the exercise with "Quality Circles", which are different in a number of ways. The groups were also in theory to consider ways in which their departmental contribution could be measured and incorporated into an incentive payment scheme.

As a result of this work, an incentive payment scheme was designed, negotiated, and agreed. The Productivity Circles began to make major changes in the way work was done in the various departments and the new top management team made other major changes such as acquiring an adjacent factory so that the layout could be completely changed.

The entire company became very closely involved in saving Kincaid's, and a new spirit of enthusiasm was born. Modular systems of manufacture were introduced; computerised management control and information systems were introduced (often where there had not even been a manual system before), and the new layout enabled a more rational flow of work to be introduced. In the midst of this, a meeting of the joint management-union organising team for the project met to discuss the new incentive bonus scheme, and in spite of the fact that another company belonging to the same Group and situated literally across the road from Kincaid's had introduced an incentive scheme paying extra money to its workforce, it was jointly agreed that Kincaid's could not afford to add to its labour costs at this time if it was to attract more orders. The incentive scheme was put on the shelf until such time as the order situation looked more healthy.

The project had been underway approximately two years when the company won the order for the engine to be installed in the replacement ship for the Atlantic Conveyor (which had been lost in the Falklands war). This engine was built in under eight months to a standard which drew a letter of congratulations from the ship's owners, and marked the company's return to its former reputation and ability.

There could be little doubt that this follow up to the research results had confirmed the findings, that consultation is far more important than the features of an incentive scheme or the matching of that scheme to contingent organisation characteristics.

However, this would suggest a very long and arduous process before any new incentive scheme could be introduced. The next step was to find out whether there are any less time-consuming ways of achieving the beneficial effects of consultation, than setting up something as fundamentally different as Productivity Circles. It is possible, for example, that well-designed interview surveys of a workforce could achieve the effect of involving them in the process of designing and implementing an incentive scheme.

The first attempts to assess this alternative approach have not yet produced conclusive results. However, it looks likely that consultation can take many forms, and that some intensive activity, such as an interview survey of a large sample and questionnaire survey of the entire staff including the shopfloor, could speed up the process considerably.

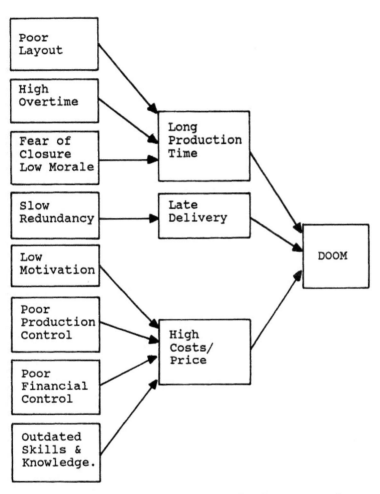

Figure 2: Problems at the beginning of action research

ANALYSING INCENTIVE PAYMENT SYSTEMS

References

Bowey, A, Thorpe, R and Helier, P: Payment Systems and Productivity Macmillan 1986.

Bowey, A: et al Effects of Incentive Payment Systems, United Kingdom. 1977-1980. Department of Employment Research paper No. 36 1982.

Legge, K: Power, Innovation and Problem Solving in Personnel Management McGraw Hill 1979.

Lupton, T: Best Fit in the Design of Organisation. Personnel Review 4. No. 1. Winter 1975.

INDEX

*For Product Safety Concerns and Information please contact
our EU representative GPSR@taylorandfrancis.com Taylor & Francis
Verlag GmbH, Kaufingerstraße 24, 80331 München, Germany*

T - #0228 - 160425 - C0 - 216/138/11 - PB - 9780415506045 - Gloss Lamination